Third Edition

CORTEZ PETERS

CHAMPIONSHIP · KEYBOARDING DRILLS

**AN INDIVIDUALIZED DIAGNOSTIC/
PRESCRIPTIVE METHOD FOR DEVELOPING
ACCURACY AND SPEED**

Cortez Peters
Undefeated Champion Typist

GLENCOE
McGraw-Hill

Photo credits—*Cover:* Morton and White Photographic; *v,* St. Louis Post–Dispatch, photo by Sam Leone; *viii,* Aaron Haupt.

Library of Congress Cataloging–in–Publication Data

Peters, Cortez.
  [Championship keyboarding drills]
  Cortez Peters' championship keyboarding drills: an individualized diagnostic and pre-scriptive method for developing accuracy and speed / Cortez Peters.—3rd ed.
    p. cm.
  Rev. ed. of: The Cortez Peters championship typing drills. 2nd ed. c1987.
  ISBN 0-02-801199-6.—ISBN 0-02-801200-3 (with disk)
  1. Keyboarding—Problems, exercises, etc. I. Peters, Cortez.
Cortez Peters championship typing drills. II. Title.
Z49.2.P48 1996   96-4343
652.3'07—dc20   CIP

Glencoe/McGraw-Hill

A Division of The **McGraw·Hill** Companies

Cortez Peters' Championship Keyboarding Drills, Third Edition

Send all inquiries to:

Glencoe/McGraw-Hill
936 Eastwind Drive
Westerville, OH 43081

ISBN 0-02-801199-6
ISBN 0-02-801200-3 with 3.5″ disk

1 2 3 4 5 6 7 8 9 RRD-W   05 04 03 02 01 00 99 98 97 96

Contents

DEDICATION

Figure 1. Cortez Peters, Champion Typist

This book is dedicated to the memory of Cortez Peters, Jr., a championship typist and the author of five typing books, who passed away June 24, 1993. He was the son of Cortez Peters, Sr., also a World Championship Typist. Cortez Peters, Jr., has left behind a legacy of love and inspiration for all of his students, motivating and urging them to persevere to achieve heights of personal success they may never have dreamed of before. He is renowned for his dedication to his craft and to the success of others. His contribution in this endeavor is sadly missed.

Author Background

Cortez Peters—The Name of Excellence in Keyboarding!

When Cortez Peters, Sr., father of the author of this book, was 15 years old, he could type 80 net words a minute (WAM) on a manual typewriter. He practiced one full year to increase his speed to 100 WAM but was unsuccessful. Then he met George Hossfield, World Typing Champion, who taught him championship keyboarding techniques. After using these techniques for only four months, Cortez Peters, Sr., became the first high school student in America to win the Platinum Pin for Excellence in Typewriting. To win this award, he had to type for 15 minutes from straight copy on a manual typewriter at the rate of 100 net words a minute without making a single error. Cortez Peters, Sr., realized from this experience that practice in and of itself does not make perfect. It is *correct* practice that makes perfect. One must practice the *correct* thing, the *correct* way, at the *correct* time in order to achieve the *correct* results.

Embracing this philosophy, Cortez Peters, Sr., went on to win the World's Amateur Typewriting Championship at the age of 18 and set a world typing record for amateur typists. In all, Mr. Peters won the World's Portable Typewriting Championship and the World's Accuracy Typewriting Championship, and he became the holder of the World's Speed Record on a manual typewriter for a 60-minute timing. In 1954, Cortez Peters, Sr., typed 184 net words a minute in zero weather while wearing mittens. This feat was authenticated in the late Bob Ripley's "Believe It or Not" column. His top speed on a 1-minute timing from straight copy was 181 net words a minute, and he typed 150 correct words a minute in 1 hour of typing from straight copy. Both records were set on a manual typewriter, and neither record has ever been broken on a nonelectric typewriter.

Cortez Peters, Sr., taught his son and the author of this program, Cortez Peters, Jr., the techniques, methods, and strategies of champion typists. It was these techniques that enabled him to become an undefeated typewriting champion in his own right. Cortez Peters, Jr., began typing at the age of 12. He participated in 12 typewriting contests and won them all. His record remains undefeated. His best speed on a 1-minute timing was 225 net words a minute; his top finger speed was 297 words a minute. Cortez Peters, Jr., was recognized as the fastest typist in the world.

to the championship typing techniques and methods that he shares with you in this skillbuilding program. This unique program of individualized diagnostic and prescriptive analysis for controlling accuracy and building speed is built on the experiences of these world championship typists.

Correct techniques are absolutely essential for acquiring championship results. The four Championship Techniques that Cortez Peters emphasizes in this program are (1) keystroking and positioning, (2) concentration, (3) rhythmic keying, and (4) conscientious practicing. His philosophy includes the following points which serve as the foundation of this program:

1. The development of Championship Techniques is essential for maintaining accuracy while building speed.
2. Rhythmic keystroking is the foundation for building speed and accuracy.
3. Errors do not happen randomly but occur in a precise, predictable pattern, and everyone's pattern is different. A diagnosis of keyboarding weaknesses should be done on an individual basis, and corrective practice for each person should be prescribed on the basis of his or her individual diagnosis.
4. Repetitive practicing, not just extensive practicing, is imperative for high speed and accuracy development.
5. Only conscientious practice of the right thing in the right way will produce the desired results.

Championship Techniques

These are the Championship Techniques that enabled Cortez Peters, Sr., and Cortez Peters, Jr., to achieve championship speeds. Study these techniques, and apply them when you key.

Keystroking and Positioning Techniques

Keystroking Techniques

Four different parts of the finger are used in championship keystroking: the finger-nail part of the finger, the fingertip, the part of the finger between the tip and the ball, and the ball of the finger. By using the four different parts of the fingers, you will be able to move only the necessary fingers (not the hands) in order to key. This will result in higher speed and better accuracy, and it is the *championship way to key.*

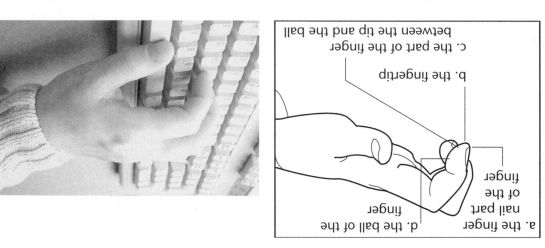

Figure 2. Parts of the finger used in keystroking

a. the finger nail part of the finger

d. the ball of the finger

b. the fingertip

c. the part of the finger between the tip and the ball

Figure 3. Hand on keyboard in "scratch-like position"

The parts of the finger described above are used in the following manner:

1. Strike the first-row keys of X, C, V, M, comma, period, Z, and the diagonal with the nail part of your finger. When you strike these first-row keys, recoil your finger. Do not move your arm or hand. Strike each of these keys with a sharp, quick downward and upward motion, and strike and release the key instantly. Return immediately to the home-row keys.

2. Strike the home-row keys (A S D F J K L ;) with the fingertips. Make a sharp, quick downward and upward motion. In spacing, use only the side of your right thumb, making a quick downward and outward motion. Strike the space bar between the B and N keys.

3. Strike the third-row keys of E, I, R, U, W, O, Q, and P with that part of your finger between the fingertip and the ball. Extend the correct finger slightly, and strike the key with a quick, sharp downward and upward motion; then return to the home-row-key position.

4. Strike the fourth-row keys (the number keys) with the balls of your fingers.
5. Strike the center keys of the first row (B and N), the second—or home—row (G and H), and the third row (T and Y) with the ball of your finger. Use a sharp, quick downward and upward motion.

Positioning Techniques

1. Center yourself to the keyboard by aligning the H key with the center of your body.
2. Place your body only a few inches from your keyboard. To determine the correct distance, curve your fingers and place them over the home-row keys, with the upper arms remaining perpendicular to the floor.
3. Keep your elbows a hand's distance from your body.
4. Keep your arms and wrists steady.
5. Sit back in your chair in a comfortable, relaxed position, with the upper part of your body leaning slightly forward.
6. Keep your feet flat on the floor, with one foot in front of the other. Never cross your legs.
7. Keep your fingers as close to the keyboard as possible. The closer the fingers are to the keys, the faster you will type.
8. Keep your fingers curved and held in a scratchlike position, with the fingertips slightly touching or hovering closely above the home-row keys.
9. Keep the upper part of each hand perfectly flat and parallel to the slope of the keyboard.
10. Keep both palms above the base of the keyboard—do not let your palms rest on the base of the keyboard.
11. Do not let your hands bounce. Move the fingers, not the hand, when you key.

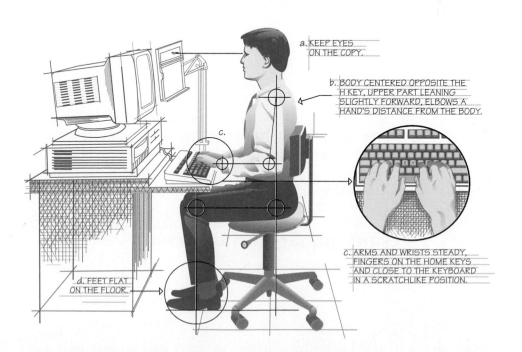

Figure 4. Positioning techniques for championship keystroking

12. Strike the space bar with your right thumb only.
13. Strike the return key by moving your right hand *slightly* to the right.
14. Keep your eyes on your copy. Do not look at your fingers or the keyboard while keying.

Concentration Techniques

1. Key for *duplication*, not comprehension, by looking only at the letters, not the words.
2. Key on a letter-for-letter (letter recognition) basis.
3. Say each letter, or spell out each word, mentally as you key it until your speed makes it impossible to do so.
4. Do not look at the keys as you type.

Rhythmic Keying Technique

Key with an easy rhythm and a smooth cadence. Students who key rhythmically key faster and more accurately than other students. The *Rhythm-Development Drills* available for this program will aid in the development of this technique.

Conscientious Practicing

1. Learn and apply the techniques that will help you build keyboarding skill.
2. Be positive and enthusiastic: believe that correct practicing of the correct materials *will* yield the desired results.
3. Practice with confidence and with purpose. Do not practice nonchalantly.
4. Do what your teacher tells you. She or he has your best interest at heart and wants to see you succeed.
5. Do the corrective drills according to the directions. Repetitive practicing is emphasized in the corrective drills because it is beneficial to building speed and controlling accuracy.

Section One

To the Student

Introduction

Cortez Peters' Championship Keyboarding Drills, **Third Edition**, is a skill enhancement program designed to upgrade keyboarding skills through technique development, individualized error analysis, and individualized prescriptive recommendations of championship typing drills to correct keystroking weaknesses. This program represents a proven concept in developing speed and accuracy at the keyboard. The keyboarding philosophy that shapes this program is derived from the author's own World Championship Typewriting background. He shares with you here the techniques, methods, and strategies that enabled him to type at the rate of 200 net words a minute.

This third edition of *Cortez Peters' Championship Keyboarding Drills* includes an Agenda of Cycle Activities, instructions to guide you through the recommended skillbuilding cycle, description and explanation of types of errors, and diagnostic charts with detailed instructions.

For your convenience, the material in this book is grouped by activity type. A description of each of the activities, including the pacing drills that are available in the **CD-ROM** component and *Rhythm-Development Tapes* package, follows.

Speed Study 10

Frequent-Shifting Sentences

DO NOT LOOK
AT YOUR
KEYBOARD

Goal: To develop fluency in using the shift key.

Features: These drill sentences contain a concentration of capital letters to compel frequent shifting. The sentences are arranged so that those requiring the most shifting are at the bottom of each drill and those requiring the least are at the top.

Line: 75 spaces, longest

Drill Assignment: These assignments are for both Pretest/Posttest and Supplemental Diagnostic Tests. For Diagnostic Test 1, use Drill 1; for Diagnostic Test 2, use Drill 2; for Diagnostic Test 3, use Drill 3; for Diagnostic Test 4, use Drill 4; and for Diagnostic Test 5, use both Drill 1 and Drill 4.

Directions: Type each line perfectly five times—not necessarily in succession, but in total. Double-space between groups of five perfect lines. Begin typing each sentence slowly, and gradually increase your typing rate as you become accustomed to the frequent shifting. Try to maintain an even typing tempo while typing accurately.

Drill 1

```
You Should Do Your Best Work At All Times To Make The Best Progress.
Typing Is Fun If You Type Well, And It Is Worth All Of Your Efforts.
Now And Then It Is True That We Can Do Well If We Want To Do So Now.
If We Enjoy Doing A Thing, We Do It As Well As It Is In Us To Do It.
It Is Up To You And Them To Find Out If He Is To Go To The Play Now.
```

Drill 2

```
Put Your Best Effort Into Learning To Key, And You Will Be Successful.
Do Your Best In Typing Each Day; You Will Be Pleased With The Results.
Now And Then It Is True That We Can Do More Than We Thought If We Try.
See If We Can Go With Them And Also Help To Do A Fine Job For The Man.
It Is The Duty Of An Aide To Do Me A Turn, And He Or She Should Do So.
```

Drill 3

```
To Master The Drills Requires Excellent Timing With Marvelous Coordination.
Practice These Drills Faithfully, And You Will Be Pleased At Your Progress.
To Develop Fluency In Your Typing Is A Satisfying And Rewarding Experience.
It Is Very Encouraging To See Your Progress In Typing Continue Every Month.
This Is A Very Difficult Drill To Master, But You Are On The Way Right Now.
```

Drill 4

```
You Should Be A Good Typist If You Follow The Paths Of Typing Champions.
Shifting Is Difficult, But You Will Succeed If You Will Continue To Try.
It Is We Who Will Have To Do Some Of The Things That We Will Not Do Now.
It Is Fine To Do Me A Big Turn And To Do It At A Time You Wish To Do So.
It Is Up To You And Me To See If It Is To Be As You And I Want It To Be.
```

Charts

The charting activities make possible the diagnosis of individual error patterns and the prescription of drills that should be keyed during corrective practice hours. Charting is absolutely essential if this program is to be followed in its intent. Four charts are provided: two to record your progress on 5-Minute Timed Writings (Chart 1) and Skill-Development Paragraphs (Chart 4) and two to record and diagnose your keystroking weaknesses and prescribe corrective practice based on the results of the 5-Minute Timed Writings (Chart 2) and Diagnostic Tests (Chart 3). Charting instructions are included with the charts. Following is a summary of the charts:

Chart 1: Speed and Accuracy Graph. This chart records your gross words a minute (GWAM) and net words a minute (NWAM) speeds from the 5-Minute Timed Writings and graphs your progress.

Chart 2: Misstroke Analysis. This chart records information from the 5-Minute Timed Writings. It classifies errors, diagnoses weaknesses in accuracy, and prescribes corrective practice for *accuracy*.

Chart 3: Speed and Accuracy Analysis. This chart records information from the Diagnostic Tests. It diagnoses weaknesses in and prescribes corrective practice for both *accuracy* and *speed*.

Chart 4: Record of Skill-Development Paragraphs. This chart records the date and speed level for each Skill-Development Paragraph keyed in 1 minute with zero errors.

Championship Warmup Drills

These drills contain basic stroke combinations and should be done on a daily basis.

5-Minute Timed Writings

There are thirty 5-Minute Timed Writings. The timed writing used in a cycle's Pretest should also be used in its Posttest. Timed writings not used in the Pretest and Posttest can be used at any time for practice and/or to measure progress. Errors from the 5-Minute Timed Writings are analyzed on the top half of Chart 2: Misstroke Analysis. Corrective practice, based on the analysis, is assigned in the bottom half of this chart. Corrective practice assignments direct the user to the appropriate drills in the Accuracy Studies.

Diagnostic Tests

The Diagnostic Tests consist of ten 1-minute timings on specially constructed sentences, each of which stresses a particular reach or stroke combination. Results are recorded on Chart 3: Speed and Accuracy Analysis. Corrective practice for *accuracy* is determined by the results recorded in the "Errors" box. Corrective practice assignments direct the user to the appropriate Accuracy Study. Corrective practice for *speed* is determined by the results recorded in the "Deficiency" box. Corrective practice assignments direct the user to the appropriate Speed Study.

Drill 3

It is up to you and me to find out if I am to go to the city for it soon.
The man is to do as he is told if he is to make a fine job with the firm.
It is the duty of a scout to do a good deed each and every day if he can.
I am to go to the store to buy some pans for a fine time we plan to have.
If you wish to type well, you will type as well as it is in you to do it.

Drill 4

See if it is to be as I say it is to be or if he is to do it as we like it.
If we like to do a task, we do it as well as it is in us to do it for them.
It is he who likes to run fast and he will run as fast as he can do so now.
You are to go to the new zoo and play with the two baby seals in the pools.
It is fine to see our speed in typing grow and it is well worth the effort.

Skill-Development Paragraphs

These 1-minute speed paragraphs range in length from 20 to 130 words a minute (WAM). The user strives to complete each paragraph in 1 minute without making a single error. Successful completion of each paragraph is recorded on Chart 4: Skill-Development Paragraphs. The Skill-Development Paragraphs should be keyed *during the last 10 minutes* of each hour of corrective practice.

Accuracy Studies

There are 27 Accuracy Studies, each of which contains a number of drills. The Accuracy Studies prescribed for corrective practice are determined from the bottom half of Chart 2 and from the "Errors" boxes of Chart 3. Accuracy Studies should be completed before Speed Studies.

Speed Studies

There are 10 Speed Studies, each of which contains a number of drills. Each Speed Study stresses different speed stroke combinations. The Speed Studies prescribed for corrective practice are determined from the "Deficiency" boxes of Chart 3. Speed Studies should be done only after Accuracy Studies from both Chart 2 and Chart 3 have been completed.

Rhythm-Development Drills (Pacing Drills)

Rhythm-Development Drills are *pacing* drills that aid you in the development of rhythmic keystroking. The drills, developed and recorded by Cortez Peters, Jr., set a predetermined keystroking pace against which you will match your own keystroking. These audio pacing drills are available on the CD-ROM component and in the *Rhythm-Development Tapes* package. They should be used after you have completed three full skillbuilding cycles and when you have achieved the GWAM (gross words a minute) speed of 35 on a 5-Minute Timed Writing. You should use the same drill for five consecutive hours, longer if your error rate is very high. Follow the drill with at least one complete skillbuilding cycle. These drills can also be used to break speed plateaus.

Speed Study 9

Frequent-Spacing Sentences

Goal: To develop fluency in using the space bar.

Features: These sentences contain a preponderance of short words to compel frequent spacing. The sentences are arranged so that those with the greatest number of words are at the top of each drill and those with the smallest number are at the bottom. Spacing between words is one of the slowest strokes in typing; therefore, if you are to become a rapid typist, you must master the art of rapid spacing.

Line: 75 spaces, longest

Drill Assignment: These assignments are for both Pretest/Posttest and Supplemental Diagnostic Tests. For Diagnostic Test 1, use Drill 1; for Diagnostic Test 2, use Drill 2; for Diagnostic Test 3, use Drill 3; for Diagnostic Test 4, use Drill 4; and for Diagnostic Test 5, use both Drill 1 and Drill 4.

Directions: Type each line perfectly five times—not necessarily in succession, but in total. Double-space between groups of five perfect lines. Start typing each sentence slowly, and gradually increase your typing rate until you are typing as fast as you can. Try to maintain an even typing tempo between striking the keys and the space bar. In striving for speed, maintain a high degree of accuracy.

Drill 1

```
I am to see if I am to do it now or if he is to do it at a later time.
It is the job of the man to help her if he can and he is to do it now.
If it is up to me to do it, I am not for it at this or any other time.
See if it is to be done now or if we can do it all in the near future.
Now and then it is true that we can do more than we thought if we try.
```

Drill 2

```
It is up to you and him to see if it is to be as you and I want it to be.
I will do it if I have to do so but I am not in it for the fun of it now.
It is the duty of a man to do me a big turn if he can and he is to do so.
It is fine to do her a big turn and to do it at a time you wish to do so.
It is she who will have to do some of the things that we will not do now.
```

How To Use This Program

This program has four components: the text, two software components (disk format or CD-ROM), and the *Rhythm-Development Tapes*. The text can be used by itself or in combination with any of the other components. Whichever combination of components you use, you have the option of using the program as supplemental drill work or as a structured skillbuilding program. Regardless of the approach you use, error identification, computations, and charting will be performed electronically if you are using the software or CD-ROM component. Otherwise, you will have to manually identify errors, perform the computations, and complete the charts. Instructions for identifying errors are on pages 8 and 9. Instructions for performing the computations and for charting accompany the charts in Section 2.

As Supplemental Drill Work. Select the activity *type* (Warmup Drills, Supplemental 5-Minute Timed Writings, Supplemental Diagnostic Tests, and so on), then specific activity. Follow the instructions for that activity. Charting, although beneficial, is optional with this approach.

As a Structured Skillbuilding Program. This is the *recommended* approach to using this program and may be done by following the "Agenda of Cycle Activities." This *cycle* approach maintains the intent and integrity of the Cortez Peters philosophy and reflects his method of building keyboarding skill.

If you are using the software or CD-ROM component, select the cycle from the menu. If you are *not* using the software or CD-ROM component, follow the "Agenda of Cycle Activities" and its accompanying instructions on pages 6–7. Suggested time allowances are given for your convenience. The following four suggestions will help you work through a cycle.

1. A skillbuilding cycle consists of certain activities performed in a specific sequence for a specified length of time. Cycle activities and their sequence should stay the same, but the length of time *allotted to each activity* and the amount of time *between each activity* may vary depending on your course schedule. A five-hour cycle is normal. Whether these five hours are all in one week or spread over several weeks depends on your course schedule. Once a cycle has been completed, it should be repeated using a different 5-Minute Timed Writing and Diagnostic Test. Repeating the cycle five consecutive times will produce the best results.

2. Use the last 10 minutes of each corrective practice hour to key the 1-minute Skill-Development Paragraphs.

3. Allow a minimum of two consecutive hours of corrective practice time between Pretest and Posttest days; three is preferred.

4. If the *Rhythm-Development Drills* are used to increase speed and accuracy through rhythmic keystroking, they should be introduced as soon as three full skillbuilding cycles have been completed *and* a GWAM speed of 35 on a 5-Minute Timed Writing has been achieved. The drills should be used for five consecutive class hours and should be *followed* by at least one complete skillbuilding cycle.

CONCENTRATE!

Drill 4

Our weak jazz boys quickly consumed extra portions of light venison.
Just six dozen brute fighters very quickly won prizes automatically.
Before subjecting the class to a quiz, Marke reviewed the xylophone.
The growing lack of jobs constitutes Quazady's major vexing problem.
Major Quinkploy was penalized five or six times because of fighting.

Drill 5

Our zeal in typing will quickly justify vexing hand mobility drills.
The fighting men very quickly zapped the black wood with jaded axes.
Mazel proudly enjoyed quiet living and existing without fried bacon.
A quick lizard vexed a jumping fox until he pawed the yellow bricks.
Queen Kalexdrica just awarded the big prize to my vanquished father.

Drill 6

A quick movement of the bold enemy will jeopardize six good divisions.
Extra work on psychology enabled five juniors to pass your major quiz.
The quiet preacher's texts just amazed forty very willing backsliders.
Zinnias, meekly vying for a bright effect, juxtaposed yellow jonquils.
The quick enzymes puzzled several exceptional judges before weakening.

Drill 7

Six typing wizards quickly amazed people just before having to leave Maine.
Very soon the boy will help make a lazy fox and quick weasel jump the gate.
The quick movement of five young elephants will jeopardize sixteen beagles.
A young, zealous Afghanistan expert very quickly believed the woman jurist.
New zigzag steps of a very quick jumping kangaroo exacerbated the old lion.

Drill 8

Our black rabbits jumped over six puzzled, very white male fighting quails.
The audacity of my buzzard was shown when he quickly vexed a jumping moose.
The old Aztec viewed our king quizzically before expertly managing to jest.
My audience was amazed by the quick, very complete, extra-revealing report.
The professor's bleak quizzes vexed many ill-prepared junior college women.

Agenda of Cycle Activities

This structured approach builds skill through the planned repetition of activities. This repetition is called a cycle—a skillbuilding cycle. Each cycle requires approximately 4 to 5 hours to complete. To achieve maximum results, a student should repeat the cycle five consecutive times.

PRETEST	CORRECTIVE PRACTICE			POSTTEST
45–60 minutes	45–60 minutes	(continued) 45–60 Minutes	(continued) 45–60 Minutes	45–60 minutes
Warmup (5′)	**Warmup (5′)**	**Warmup (5′)**	**Warmup (5′)**	**Warmup (5′)**
Pretest 5-Minute Timed Writing Diagnostic Test	Key the prescribed Accuracy Studies from Chart 2.	Key the prescribed Accuracy Studies from Chart 2 if not finished. or	Key the prescribed Accuracy Studies from Chart 2 if not finished. or	**Posttest** 5-Minute Timed Writing Diagnostic Test
Record Results Record results of the 5-Minute Timed Writing on Chart 1 and Chart 2.	Key the prescribed Accuracy Studies from Chart 3 when all assignments from Chart 2 have been completed.	Key the prescribed Accuracy Studies from Chart 3 when all assignments from Chart 2 have been completed. or	Key the prescribed Accuracy Studies from Chart 3 when all assignments from Chart 2 have been completed. or	**Record Results** Record results of the 5-Minute Timed Writing on Chart 1 and *the top part only* of Chart 2.
Prioritize the prescribed corrective practice on Chart 2.	Key the prescribed Speed Studies from Chart 3.	Key the prescribed Speed Studies from Chart 3 when all assignments from Chart 2 are completed and all Accuracy Studies assignments for Chart 3 are completed.	Key the prescribed Speed Studies from Chart 3 when all assignments from Chart 2 are completed and all Accuracy Studies assignments for Chart 3 are completed.	Record results of the Diagnostic Test on Chart 3.
Record results of the Diagnostic Test on Chart 3.	Key Skill-Development Paragraphs during the last 10 minutes.	Key Skill-Development Paragraphs during the last 10 minutes.	Key Skill-Development Paragraphs during the last 10 minutes.	*Compare the Posttest results with the Pretest results.*
Prioritize the prescribed corrective practice on Chart 3.	**Record Results** Record Skill-Development Paragraphs on Chart 4.	**Record Results** Record Skill-Development Paragraphs on Chart 4.	**Record Results** Record Skill-Development Paragraphs on Chart 4.	

Speed Study 8

Alphabetic Sentences

Goal: To develop fluency in typing the entire alphabet.

Features: These sentences, each of which contains the 26 letters of the alphabet, are arranged in order of difficulty, with the least difficult at the top of each drill and the most difficult at the bottom.

Line: 75 spaces, longest

Drill Assignment: These assignments are for both Pretest/Posttest and Supplemental Diagnostic Tests. For Diagnostic Test 1, use Drill 1; for Diagnostic Test 2, use Drill 2; for Diagnostic Test 3, use both Drill 3 and Drill 6; for Diagnostic Test 4, use both Drill 4 and Drill 7; and for Diagnostic Test 5, use both Drill 5 and Drill 8.

Directions: Type each line perfectly five times—not necessarily in succession, but in total. Double-space between groups of five perfect lines. Begin typing each sentence at a slow rate of speed, and gradually increase your typing rate until you are able to type it at your most rapid accurate rate.

Drill 1

The very quick typing expert just amazed our willing buffoons.

Two quick brown foxes jumped over the youngest sleeping zebra.

Their jazz expert can quickly manage to weave fabulous sounds.

Our six jumping zebras very quickly forced Harvey to withdraw.

Our lynx and zebra very quickly jumped over the wheezing frog.

Drill 2

Just four dozen boxes were moved quietly by carefully packing them.

Our famous gray squirrels jeopardized their very next black walnut.

Two black jets zipped quietly before many very highly waxed planes.

Their zebras jumped over six black squirrels following your trails.

Five or six cartons were awarded as equal major prizes by a knight.

Drill 3

Mr. Quicke extrapolated the many hazards involved by joining waifs.

Your waltz quickly amazed Jeff and Steve plus excited bright folks.

Vabor's jasmine fragrance very quickly excels prize-winning aromas.

The very quaint woman just amazed Captain Vexoray by killing gnats.

Their seven boxes of paper quickly disquieted Thomas Z. Wright, Jr.

Agenda of Cycle Activities

Begin each day with Warmup Drills for 5 minutes.

Pretest (45–60 minutes)

1. Take two attempts on a Pretest/Posttest 5-Minute Timed Writing (Pretest/Posttest Timed Writing 1 for the first time through the cycle, Pretest/Posttest Timed Writing 2 for the second time through the cycle, and so on). Follow the directions given in the 5-Minute Timed Writings section (Section 4).

2. For each attempt:
   a. Determine the total number of words keyed in 5 minutes. Note the word count next to the last *complete* line keyed, and add the incomplete line by using the scale at the bottom of the timing.
   b. Compute the gross words a minute (GWAM) speed: divide the number of words keyed (the total from *a* above) by the number of minutes in the timing, in this case 5. Round off this result, if necessary.
   c. Circle your errors, and determine the total number of errors made.
   d. Compute the net words a minute (NWAM) speed: GWAM speed minus 2 words (or points) for each error. Round off this result, if necessary.

3. Compare the results of the two 5-Minute Timed Writings, and select the better of the two for charting purposes. Use the following guidelines to select the better timing:
   a. If both attempts had 5 errors or less, select the one with the higher NWAM speed. If the NWAM speeds are equal, select the timed writing with fewer errors.
   b. If both attempts had more than 5 errors, select the one with fewer errors.
   c. If one attempt had 5 errors or less and the other attempt had more than 5 errors, select the one with 5 errors or less.

4. Take the Diagnostic Test (Pretest/Posttest Diagnostic Test 1 for the first time through the cycle, Pretest/Posttest Diagnostic Test 2 for the second time through the cycle, and so on. Repeat the sequence of Diagnostic Test 1 through Diagnostic Test 5 for cycles 6 through 10.). Follow the directions given in the Diagnostic Tests section (Section 5). Key each sentence as many times as you can in 1 minute.

5. For each sentence:
   a. Compute the gross words a minute (GWAM) speed. Each line has 14 words. Multiply the number of *complete* lines by 14, and add the number of additional words from the incomplete line by using the scale at the bottom of the timing.
   b. Circle your errors, and determine the total number of errors made.
   c. Compute the correct words a minute (CWAM) speed: GWAM speed minus 1 word (or point) for each error. Round off this result, if necessary.

6. Record Pretest results:
   a. Record the results of the selected 5-Minute Timed Writing on Charts 1 and 2. Follow the instructions for each of the charts.
   b. Record the results of the Diagnostic Test in the Pretest column of each sentence on Chart 3. Follow the instructions for the chart.

Drill 4

The organized mink monopoly is the greatest fear of the wealthy women.
Two glassy-eyed statesmen stared as if they were in a vegetated state.
Some oily barges looked to be deserted of even minimum human activity.
An ill pupil fell into the oily pool as she dared to walk on its edge.
My nylon dress was the best garb she could wear to the bazaar at noon.

Drill 5

Our popular people always pull the greatest gates at their best affairs.
The decedent had deeded an oil well to you a few weeks before his death.
A quick look at our lions deterred the pupil with tears from joining us.
An Egyptian mummy started a craze in archaeology that exceeded my hopes.
Minimum wages grew and grew steadily over the last decade in my opinion.

Corrective Practice (45–60 minutes, three consecutive times)

1. Key the Accuracy Studies prescribed in Chart 2 in the sequence you have indicated. Turn to the Accuracy Studies section (Section 7), select the appropriate Accuracy Study and/or drill number, and follow the directions. After you complete an Accuracy Study or drill, return to Chart 2 and draw an "X" through the sequence number that assigned that study or drill.

2. Key the Accuracy Studies prescribed from the "Errors" box in Chart 3 in the sequence you have indicated. Turn to the Accuracy Studies section (Section 7), select the appropriate Accuracy Study and/or drill number, and follow the directions. After you complete an Accuracy Study or drill, return to Chart 3 and draw an "X" through the "Errors" box that assigned that study or drill.

3. Key the Speed Studies prescribed from the "Deficiency" box in Chart 3 in the sequence you have indicated. Turn to the Speed Studies section (Section 8), select the appropriate Speed Study and/or drill number, and follow the directions. After you complete a Speed Study or drill, return to Chart 3 and draw an "X" through the "Deficiency" box that assigned that study or drill.

4. Key the 1-minute Skill-Development Paragraphs during the last 10 minutes of each hour of corrective practice, following the directions for that section (Section 6). The number of attempts you are allowed each day will be determined by your teacher.

5. Record your progress on Chart 4. Each time you key a paragraph in 1 minute without making a single error, fill in that paragraph's circle on the chart and proceed to the next paragraph. Follow the instructions on the chart.

Posttest (45–60 minutes)

1. Take two attempts on the same 5-Minute Timed Writing that was used in the Pretest.

2. For each attempt:
   a. Determine the total number of words keyed in the 5 minutes.
   b. Compute the gross words a minute (GWAM) speed.
   c. Circle your errors, and determine the total number of errors made.
   d. Compute the net words a minute (NWAM) speed.

3. Compare the results of the two 5-Minute Timed Writings, and using the guidelines under "Pretest", select the better of the two for charting.

4. Take the same Diagnostic Test that was used in the Pretest.

5. For each sentence:
   a. Compute the GWAM speed.
   b. Circle your errors, and determine the total number of errors made.
   c. Compute the CWAM speed.

6. Record Posttest results:
   a. Record the results of the selected 5-Minute Timed Writing on Chart 1 and *the top part only* of Chart 2. No corrective practice will be assigned from Chart 2, so it is not necessary to fill in the bottom half of the chart.
   b. Record the results of the Diagnostic Test in the Posttest column of each sentence on Chart 3.

7. *Compare the results of the Posttest with those of the Pretest.*

NOTE: The *Rhythm-Development Drills* may be used between the third and fourth or fourth and fifth repetitions of a cycle.

Speed Study 7

One-Hand-Word Sentences

Goal: To develop fluency in typing one-hand words.

Features: These sentences contain a concentration of one-hand words and are arranged so that those containing the smallest number of one-hand words are at the top of each drill, while those with a greater number of them are at the bottom.

Line: 75 spaces, longest

Drill Assignment: These assignments are for both Pretest/Posttest and Supplemental Diagnostic Tests. For Diagnostic Test 1, use Drill 1; for Diagnostic Test 2, use Drill 2; for Diagnostic Test 3, use Drill 3; for Diagnostic Test 4, use Drill 4; and for Diagnostic Test 5, use Drill 5.

Directions: Type each line perfectly five times—not necessarily in succession, but in total. Double-space between groups of five perfect lines. Start typing each sentence slowly, and gradually increase your typing rate until you are able to type at your fastest accurate speed.

Drill 1

Your deer veered in the field and retreated into the rear garage.

The tax rebates started the economy on an upturn as was assessed.

The Desert Fox was steadfast in his rear-guard retreat in Africa.

Our fat cat scattered garbage upon my garage floor and retreated.

A puny puppy chased a crazed cat in the grass area of the crater.

Drill 2

The pink pin was not union-made and badly ripped the nylon garment.

Their red bear was eager to tear the beehive down from the treetop.

Our jolly, bearded redhead jumped over the bag and tested your car.

Only our pumpkin and onion were the best in the opinion of experts.

Your dazed bear raged in his cage as a lion slyly looked on nearby.

Drill 3

Your monopoly started the hula-hoop craze that swept our great nation.

The Arab oil embargos started a great gas war that upset many nations.

His steadfast refusal to accede exceeded the opinion of our jolly dad.

Their eager pupil dared to weave an inky pattern upon sassafras paper.

Our well-fed polo pony only stared at a puny onion in his small stall.

Identifying Errors

If you are using one of the software components, errors will be identified and classified electronically. If you are *not* using the software component, you will need to know what constitutes an error and how to classify it. If more than one error is made in a word, only the first error is counted. When evaluating a word for errors, consider the spelling of the word and the space or the punctuation and space following that word. Considering the punctuation and spacing that follows the word as part of the word allows for the recognition of punctuation and spacing errors.

There are five *categories* of errors: letter misstrokes, punctuation errors, shifting errors, spacing errors, and concentration errors. Each category of errors is described below.

1. *Letter Misstrokes.* A letter misstroke occurs when a letter, punctuation mark, or space is keyed in *place of* the correct letter.

   `went: weit    we't    we t`

2. *Punctuation Errors.* A punctuation error occurs when the wrong punctuation mark is keyed or a punctuation mark is omitted.

   `don't: don"t    dont`

3. *Shifting Errors.* A shifting error occurs when a letter is keyed in the wrong case.

   `boy: Boy    bOy`

4. *Spacing Errors.* A spacing error occurs when a space is replaced by a letter or punctuation mark, when a space is added within a word, when an extra space is added between words, or when a space is omitted.

   `The dog ran.: Theedog ran.    The'dog ran.    T he dog ran.`

   `The  dog ran.    Thedog ran.`

5. *Concentration Errors.* There are four kinds of concentration errors: transpositions, omissions, additions, and doubling the wrong letter. When the first letters of these words are combined, they spell **TOAD.** TOAD is an acronym for **T**ransposition, **O**mission, **A**ddition, and **D**oubling the wrong letter. This acronym will help you remember which kinds of errors are concentration errors.

   a. *Transposition.* Two letters are transposed with each other.

   `phone: phnoe    hpone`

   b. *Omission.* A letter is omitted from a word.

   `phone: phne    phon`

   c. *Addition.* A letter or punctuation mark is added to a word.

   `phone: phones    pho,ne`

   d. *Doubling the wrong letter.* In a word that contains a double-letter pattern, the wrong letter is doubled.

   `letter: leeter    lleter    leterr`

Drill 4

A baggage official alleges that the supply of lizard skins is worrisome.
It appears, to my horror, that a terrible error will add to our problem.
The aberration embarrassed and deterred the sweet, opportunistic fellow.
Our bookkeeper struggled all week, under pressure, to balance his books.
Anne took the book and looked for a different summary to tell the class.

Drill 5

Our groggy, staggering bullfighter assailed the old bull with all his fury.
An odd rabbit lopped a lizard, attacked a cabbage, and bobbed up your hill.
It is difficult for your bookkeeper to meet all committee rules officially.
My coffee connoisseur succeeded in accounting for the low supply of coffee.
A helpless raccoon successfully embarrassed an angry, aggressive bullmoose.

Sample sentence: The boy went to the store, but his three sisters were not allowed to go with him.

                  1   2   3 4   5   6   7   8

Keyed incorrectly: The biy went to the store; but His three sistres wee not' aloweed to go with him.

Diagnosis of the above errors:

1. Letter misstroke: the letter *i* was keyed in place of *o*.
2. Punctuation error: a semicolon (;) was keyed in place of the comma (,).
3. Shifting error: an uppercase *H* was keyed instead of the lowercase *h*.
4. Spacing error: an extra space was added between *his* and *three*.
5. Transposition (concentration) error: the letters *e* and *r* were transposed.
6. Omission (concentration) error: the letter *r* was omitted.
7. Addition (concentration) error: a punctuation mark was added to the word *not*.
8. Doubling the wrong letter (concentration): the letter *e* was doubled instead of the letter *l*.

Speed Study 6

Double-Letter Sentences

KEEP EYES ON COPY

Goal: To develop fluency in making double-letter strokes.

Features: These sentences contain a preponderance of double-letter words and are arranged so that those containing the smallest number of double-letter words are at the top of each drill, while those containing a greater concentration of them are at the bottom. Double-letter strokes are among the slowest and most difficult stroke combinations in typing, especially at the high-speed level.

Line: 75 spaces, longest

Drill Assignment: These assignments are for both Pretest/Posttest and Supplemental Diagnostic Tests. For Diagnostic Test 1, use Drill 1; for Diagnostic Test 2, use Drill 2; for Diagnostic Test 3, use Drill 3; for Diagnostic Test 4, use Drill 4; and for Diagnostic Test 5, use Drill 5.

Directions: Type each line perfectly five times—not necessarily in succession, but in total. Double-space between groups of five perfect lines. Begin typing each sentence slowly, and gradually increase your typing speed until you reach your fastest accurate rate.

Drill 1

Your summaries took a week to account for the missing items.

The buzzard puzzled and dazzled the bobbing, hopping rabbit.

The careless and embarrassed robber assists the puzzled man.

Our letter will make it less difficult to find a bookkeeper.

A good queen will add class in running her official affairs.

Drill 2

Your engineers assume that a discussion of stress will be helpful.

It appears that our supply of wrapped puzzles exceeded the demand.

A good broom will sweep the floor very clean at every opportunity.

The football rally filled the hall and helped in winning the game.

Your jazz rally really affected the jamming, skinny fiddle player.

Drill 3

The computer programmer really communicated better after the occasion.

Our dollar bill today looks less stable as the international currency.

I recommend summarizing the communication to attract better attention.

The class quiz succeeded in getting a little better attention from us.

Our smaller malls will meet community demands sooner than bigger ones.

Section Two

Diagnostic Charts

The diagnostic charts on the following pages are used to record the results of the 5-Minute Timed Writings, the Diagnostic Test sentences, and the Skill-Development Paragraphs. Two charts *record speed and accuracy progress:* Chart 1 graphs your progress on the 5-Minute Timed Writings, and Chart 4 records each successful completion of the 1-minute Skill-Development Paragraphs. Two other charts *detect error patterns* and *prescribe corrective practice:* Chart 2 detects problems in accuracy and assigns corrective practice on Accuracy Studies; Chart 3 detects problems in speed as well as accuracy and assigns corrective practice on both Speed Studies and Accuracy Studies.

All charts may be duplicated for use with this program.

Drill 4

A sweet fragrance drifted through the fresh air and brought gratification.
Your azalea and mum bazaars attracted numerous friends from various areas.
An eccentric recluse decided to dedicate an aquaplane for his jolly nurse.
Your crafty grocer deeded a swamp to a brave graduate and tax-deducted it.
Their nylon umbrella overburdened the hungry celebrity eating gingerbread.

Drill 5

The old nylon kimono softened a friend's frame and enhanced her appearance.
Many unnumbered aluminum targets have now been accumulated at the aquarium.
An old, grumpy grizzly bear grazed on cool grass and viewed lizards nearby.
The lonely mystic hugged a gregarious old Aztec and pledged his friendship.
A soliloquy brought a swelter of unkind, derisive grimaces from the colony.

Chart 1: Speed and Accuracy Graph for 5-Minute Timed Writings

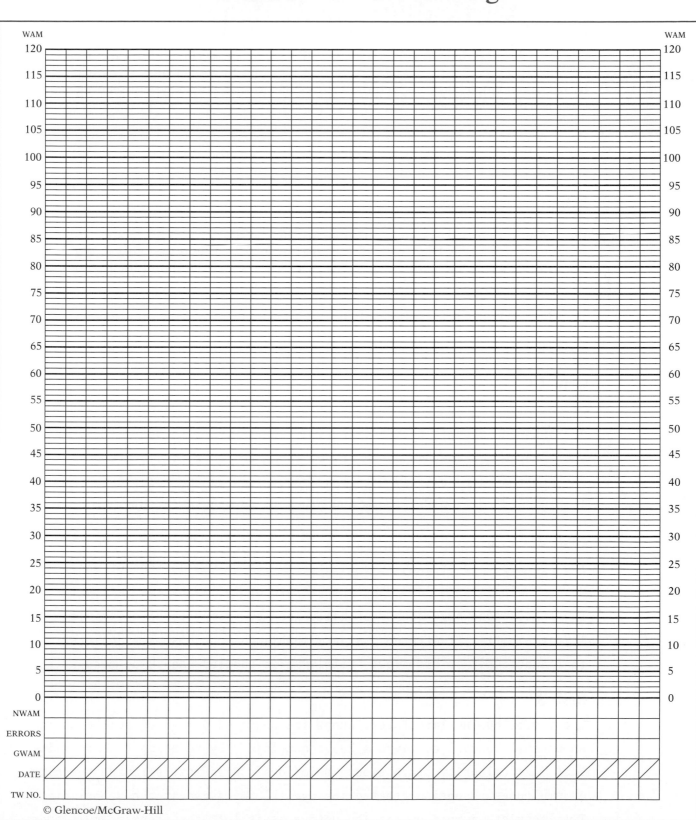

Speed Study 5

Vertical-Stroke Sentences

KEEP FINGERS CURVED.

Goal: To develop fluency in making vertical strokes. A vertical stroke is involved when two or more consecutive strokes are made by the same finger on different rows of the keyboard; for example, *my,* in which the J finger has to strike two keys consecutively on different rows of the keyboard.

Features: These sentences contain a concentration of vertical-stroke words and are arranged so that those with the smallest number of vertical strokes are at the top of each drill, while those with the greatest number are at the bottom.

Line: 75 spaces, longest

Drill Assignment: These assignments are for both Pretest/Posttest and Supplemental Diagnostic Tests. For Diagnostic Test 1, use Drill 1; for Diagnostic Test 2, use Drill 2; for Diagnostic Test 3, use Drill 3; for Diagnostic Test 4, use Drill 4; and for Diagnostic Test 5, use Drill 5.

Directions: Type each line perfectly five times—not necessarily in succession, but in total. Double-space between groups of five perfect lines. Begin typing each sentence slowly, and gradually increase your typing rate until you reach your maximum accurate typing speed.

Drill 1

Our kickers injured and bruised their fragile frames in blizzards.

Any inhumane pledges decidedly portray some barbarism in humanity.

That braggart chews his fresh, sweet fruit and bows to his granny.

The craft drifted swiftly with the smooth flow of the muddy brook.

A very cold swan swiftly swam the brook to celebrate its birthday.

Drill 2

The red lobsters broiled in a light-gray pot to the delight of many.

My immunologists decided that an outbreak of influenza was imminent.

The state ceded huge grants of hilly land to grumpy local officials.

A gray kibitzer frustrated the jury mumbling about his many junkets.

Your annual bazaar has grown swiftly as it dazzled many kind people.

Drill 3

The mysterious nuclear threat numbs the logic of our grave deliberations.

An unusual buzzard survived a hazardous injury by reducing some activity.

That jazz celebrity blows sweet, melodious sounds that serenade humanity.

A tumultuous reception greeted the cynical mortgagee at the school plaza.

Two lobbyists jumped on the locomotive as it left the frenzied multitude.

Speed and Accuracy Graph

Chart 1 on page 11 records information from the 5-Minute Timed Writings. It graphs the progress made in both speed and accuracy.

Instructions for using the Speed and Accuracy Graph follow:

1. Enter the timed writing number at the bottom of the chart, and record the date.

2. Record your gross words a minute (GWAM) speed; that is, total words keyed divided by 5 (rounded off).

3. Record the number of errors.

4. Compute and record your net words a minute (NWAM) speed; that is, GWAM speed minus a 2-word penalty for each error.

5. Plot the GWAM speed on the graph by placing a dot in the center of the column on the line corresponding to your GWAM speed.

6. Plot the NWAM speed by placing another dot in the center of the column on the line corresponding to your NWAM speed. The first time you plot the speeds, identify each dot as GWAM or NWAM in the margin to the left of the graph. If your GWAM and NWAM speeds are the same (because you made no errors), use only *one* dot to reflect both speeds.

7. Graph (connect the dots) after Timed Writing 2 has been recorded.

Figure 5 shows an example of graphed scores.

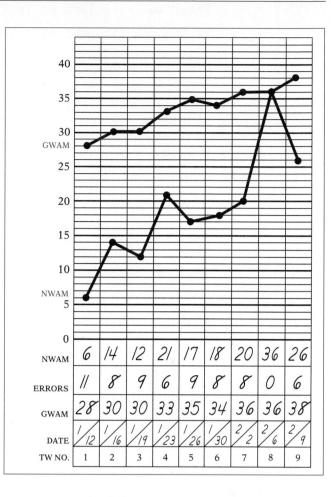

Figure 5. Example of Chart 1

NWAM	6	14	12	21	17	18	20	36	26
ERRORS	11	8	9	6	9	8	8	0	6
GWAM	28	30	30	33	35	34	36	36	38
DATE	1/12	1/16	1/19	1/23	1/26	1/30	2/2	2/6	2/9
TW NO.	1	2	3	4	5	6	7	8	9

Drill 3

The piano will last as long as the quiet boy plays it in a fine way.
No one can find out more about the future than by studying the past.
Diagnostic typing can enable you to improve your speed and accuracy.
The girl displayed poise as she went on her way home that sunny day.
Be sure that when you practice typing, you do it with a lot of zest.

Drill 4

Work on your typing with daily regularity in a well-developed program.
I can find out what happened if you fail to pick up the last ten boys.
The ship sailed out of the port into the open sea without the captain.
To ignore the methods of typing champions will lead you to mediocrity.
The good personality of the girl helped make her a very famous person.

Drill 5

He might take the option on the house if proper financing can be found.
One can endure rain quite well if one has the means to find a dry spot.
There might be more jobs for everyone in the country if we plan for it.
She may fail to cure a cold but a female may get well if she gets rest.
More and more boys and girls find that proficiency comes with practice.

NAME _____

Chart 2: Misstroke Analysis for 5-Minute Timed Writings

Sequence of Corrective Practice Drills

1. Concentration
2. Letters of the Alphabet
3. Punctuation, Shifting, and Spacing
4. Fingers
5. Hands
6. Total Errors

*CONCENTRATION DRILL SCHEDULE

For Cycle Number	Accuracy Study Number
1	22 and 23
2	24
3	25*
4	26 and 24
5	27*
6 on…	Repeat the sequence

* = Backwards

LETTERS OF THE ALPHABET

Left-Hand Keys / Right-Hand Keys

		Left-Hand Keys									Right-Hand Keys									
	4th Finger	3rd Finger	2nd Finger	1st Finger					1st Finger					2nd Finger	3rd Finger	4th Finger				
	Q A	Z	W S	X E D	C R F V T G	B Y	H N U J	M	I K	O L	P										

LEFT-HAND ERROR SUMMARY
Finger

4th	3rd	2nd	1st	Total Left
1	2	2	3	4
17	15	13	11	19

RIGHT-HAND ERROR SUMMARY
Finger

1st	2nd	3rd	4th	Total Right
3	2	2	1	4
12	14	16	18	20

Punctuation Errors	Shifting Errors	Spacing Errors	Concentration Errors	Total Errors
1	1	1	2	5
21	10	9	•	7

TIMED WRITING NUMBER

ACCURACY STUDY 8

Drill Numbers for Accuracy Study 8:

Max. Errors Allowed	1	2	2	3	4	1	1	1	1	1	1	1	1	1	1	1	1	1	1	1	1	1	1	1	1	1	1	1	1
Accuracy Study	17	26	23	19	24	5	4	3	18	6	22	20	7	2	25	8	14	21	10	13	9	11	15	12	1	16			

TW No.___
TW No.___
TW No.___
TW No.___
TW No.___
TW No.___
TW No.___
TW No.___
TW No.___

Speed Study 4

Compound-and Multiple-Stroke Sentences

STRIKE SPACE
BAR WITH
RIGHT THUMB

Goal: To develop fluency in making compound- and multiple-stroke combinations. A compound stroke is one in which two or more consecutive strokes are made by two or more different fingers of the same hand; for example, the word *not,* in which the letters *no* are struck by two different fingers of the right hand. A multiple stroke takes place when two compound strokes in one word involve two or more fingers of one hand and then two or more fingers of the other hand. Example: *more,* which involves two fingers of the right hand, followed by two fingers of the left hand. You can develop tremendous typing speed by mastering compound and multiple strokes.

Features: These sentences contain a preponderance of compound- and multiple-stroke words. The sentences are arranged so that those with the greatest number of compound strokes are at the top of each drill and those with the smallest number are at the bottom.

Line: 75 spaces, longest

Drill Assignment: These assignments are for both Pretest/Posttest and Supplemental Diagnostic Tests. For Diagnostic Test 1, use Drill 1; for Diagnostic Test 2, use Drill 2; for Diagnostic Test 3, use Drill 3; for Diagnostic Test 4, use Drill 4; and for Diagnostic Test 5, use Drill 5.

Directions: Type each line perfectly five times—not necessarily in succession, but in total. Double-space between groups of five perfect lines. Start typing each line slowly, gradually increasing your typing rate on each line until you are able to type at your maximum accurate speed.

Drill 1

The pure vein of silver was more than we had anticipated at first.

We find that our view is not in harmony with that of some friends.

Now and then he could pick out a fine tune on his brand new piano.

Josie can hit the ball hard if it is pitched to her favorite spot.

The lure of the lost wilds called many boys and men to a new life.

Drill 2

Whether we find more shops can make a big change in our selections.

He failed to find news about the job situation in his own hometown.

The paint can be picked off the post daily and thrown into the pit.

He might view the situation with some concern, but for his options.

One must try to do the best work every day to win fame and fortune.

Chart 2 on page 13 classifies the errors made on the 5-Minute Timed Writings. Further, it identifies keystroking weaknesses and error patterns and prescribes corrective practice on the Accuracy Studies based on these results. An example of recording on the chart is shown on page 15.

Top Part of Chart 2
(Diagnosing Accuracy Errors)

1. In the Timed Writing Number column, record the timed writing number for which you are posting results.

2. Classify and record errors made on the *letters of the alphabet.* Locate the heading "Letters of the Alphabet." Notice that all keys are classified as either left-hand or right-hand keys. In the box under each letter on which you made an error, record the letter that you keyed in error.

3. Classify and record errors made in *punctuation, shifting, spacing,* and *concentration* (transposition, omission, addition, and doubling the wrong letter) by placing a dot in the appropriate box for each time an error was made in that category. For example, if you made five shifting errors in your timed writing, then there would be five dots in the "Shifting" box.

4. Compute the total number of errors made by each finger of each hand.
   a. Beginning with "Left-Hand Keys" under "Letters of the Alphabet," total the errors made by individual fingers, and record each total in the appropriate finger column under the "Left-Hand Error Summary" heading. For example, if you made three errors on the letter *W,* record the number 3 in the 3rd finger box under Left-Hand Error Summary.
   b. Repeat this process for "Right-Hand Keys" under "Letters of the Alphabet."

5. Compute the total number of errors made by each hand.
   a. Add the totals in each of the finger columns under the "Left-Hand Error Summary" heading, and record this total in the "Total Left" column.
   b. Add the totals in each of the finger columns under the "Right-Hand Error Summary" heading, and record this total in the "Total Right" column under the "Right-Hand Error Summary" heading.

6. Compute the total errors by adding the numbers in the "Total Left" column (under "Left-Hand Error Summary"), the "Total Right" column (under "Right-Hand Error Summary"), the "Punctuation Errors" column, the "Shifting Errors" column, the "Spacing Errors" column, and the "Concentration Errors" column. Record this total in the "Total Errors" column, located on the far right side of the chart.

Bottom Part of Chart 2
(Prescribing Corrective Practice on Accuracy Studies)

The bottom half of this chart prescribes the Accuracy Studies or Accuracy Study and drill that should be keyed during the time allotted for corrective practice. For example, if you made three errors on the letter *W,* record the number 3 in the 3rd finger box under Left-Hand Error Summary.

1. In the Timed Writing Number column, record the timed writing number for which you are posting results.

2. Place a dot in each column where the number of errors made (top half of the chart) exceeds the maximum number of errors allowed (bottom half of the chart). These are the areas in which you need corrective practice for accuracy.

3. Prioritize the sequence in which corrective practice from this chart should be done by placing a number in each box that contains a dot. Place the number over the dot. The sequence should be prioritized in this order:

   Concentration errors (always first)

   Letters-of-the-alphabet errors (those letters with the most errors first)

   Punctuation, shifting, and spacing errors

   Finger errors (under the "Left-Hand Error Summary" and "Right-Hand Error Summary" headings)

   Hand errors ("Total Left" column under the "Left-Hand Error Summary" heading and "Total Right" column under the "Right-Hand Error Summary" heading)

   Total errors (always last)

Drill 4

Their ancient ivory emblem is an ornament to enrich and endow the city.
The height of the chapel may profit the land value of the neighborhood.
The big wolf makes a run for her lair and lays down with her pale cubs.
The authenticity of the proxy votes did torment the lame-duck official.
If I focus on the dormant social problems, I will dismay our neighbors.

Drill 5

The girl on a bicycle made a right-angle turn on a busy lane in the city.
It is right to go to socials if they wish to mingle with their neighbors.
An ambush on the right flank of the corps may dismay their ill commander.
Did our neurotic neighbor enliven the sorority with her trivial problems?
Your auditor lays the blame for the penalties on a fiendish, bogus audit.

LETTERS OF THE ALPHABET

Figure 6. Top part of Chart 2

TIMED WRITING NUMBER	Left-Hand Keys																Right-Hand Keys										LEFT-HAND ERROR SUMMARY					RIGHT-HAND ERROR SUMMARY					Punctuation Errors	Shifting Errors	Spacing Errors	Concentration Errors	Total Errors
	4th Finger			3rd Finger			2nd Finger			1st Finger						1st Finger						2nd Finger		3rd Finger		4th Finger	Finger				Total Left	Finger				Total Right					
	Q	A	Z	W	S	X	E	D	C	R	F	V	T	G	B	Y	H	N	U	J	M	I	K	O	L	P	4th	3rd	2nd	1st		1st	2nd	3rd	4th						
1					l					t				y								o		u			.	1		4	5	1	1	1		2	.	:	.	:	15

Figure 7. Bottom part of Chart 2

ACCURACY STUDY 8 — Drill Number for Accuracy Study 8:

	Q	A	Z	W	S	X	E	D	C	R	F	V	T	G	B	Y	H	N	U	J	M	I	K	O	L	P	4th	3rd	2nd	1st	Tot L	1st	2nd	3rd	4th	Tot R	Punct.	Shift	Space	Conc.	Total
Max. Errors Allowed	1	1	1	1	1	1	1	1	1	1	1	1	1	1	1	1	1	1	1	1	1	1	1	1	1	1	1	2	2	3	4	3	2	2	1	4	1	1	1	2	5
Accuracy Study	17	1	26	23	19	24	5	4	3	18	6	22	20	7	2	25	8	14	21	10	13	9	11	15	12	16	17	15	13	11	19	12	14	16	18	20	21	10	9	*	7

Handwritten sequence markings: *1, *2 (at 22), *3, *4 (at 15), *5 (at 19), *6

TW No. 1												*2																			*5						*3		*1	*6
TW No. ___																																									
TW No. ___																																									
TW No. ___																																									
TW No. ___																																									
TW No. ___																																									
TW No. ___																																									
TW No. ___																																									
TW No. ___																																									

©Glencoe/McGraw-Hill

Sequence of Corrective Practice Drills

1. Concentration
2. Letters of the Alphabet
3. Punctuation, Shifting, and Spacing
4. Fingers
5. Hands
6. Total Errors

*CONCENTRATION DRILL SCHEDULE

For Cycle Number	Accuracy Study Number
1	22 and 23
2	24
3	25*
4	26 and 24
5	27*
6 on...	Repeat the sequence

* = Backwards

Speed Study 3

Alternate-Hand Sentences

FINGERS CLOSE TO THE KEYBOARD

Goal: To develop fluency in alternating hands while typing.

Features: These sentences contain a preponderance of alternate-hand words and are arranged so that those with the greatest number of alternate-hand words are at the top of each drill, while those with the smallest number are at the bottom.

Line: 75 spaces, longest

Drill Assignment: These assignments are for both Pretest/Posttest and Supplemental Diagnostic Tests. For Diagnostic Test 1, use Drill 1; for Diagnostic Test 2, use Drill 2; for Diagnostic Test 3, use Drill 3; for Diagnostic Test 4, use Drill 4; and for Diagnostic Test 5, use Drill 5.

Directions: Type each line perfectly five times—not necessarily in succession, but in total. Double-space between groups of five perfect lines. Begin typing each line slowly; gradually increase your typing rate on each line until you are able to type as fast as you can with accuracy.

Drill 1

A giant whale is a sight to enchant the visitor and neighbors.

Henry cut the handle of the memento with an antique ivory pen.

The gowns of the girls dismayed the social clan of rich girls.

A busy, rich man got a big turkey and threw it some pale corn.

Bob wishes to augment their handiwork by the aid of ornaments.

Drill 2

The boy wishes to fish with a rod in a dismal lake with a neighbor.

The prodigy is an authentic giant in the field of ancient toxicity.

Clemency may be a civic problem if it is not handled the right way.

Their auto burial firm pays fair prices for the worn autos it buys.

Eighty turkeys may make a big profit for busy Alan and his friends.

Drill 3

He is to fix the auto panels and mend the hoses if he is to get paid.

Your bright neighbor has a very rigid view of what is right or wrong.

An unusual blend of fish and clams may fix a fair price for the meal.

This neurotic visitor may bring down the six docks if he is not paid.

The lament of the pilots was a visible sight that saddened the world.

Chart 3: Speed and Accuracy Analysis for Diagnostic Tests

ITEM	Sentence 1		Sentence 2		Sentence 3		Sentence 4		Sentence 5		Sentence 6		Sentence 7		Sentence 8		Sentence 9		Sentence 10	
	PRE	POST	PRE	POST	PRE	POST	PRE	POST	PRE	POST	PRE	POST	PRE	POST	PRE	POST	PRE	POST	PRE	POST
Diagnostic Test 1 — Errors																				
Minimum																				
CWAM																				
Deficiency																				
Diagnostic Test 2 — Errors																				
Minimum																				
CWAM																				
Deficiency																				
Diagnostic Test 3 — Errors																				
Minimum																				
CWAM																				
Deficiency																				
Diagnostic Test 4 — Errors																				
Minimum																				
CWAM																				
Deficiency																				
Diagnostic Test 5 — Errors																				
Minimum																				
CWAM																				
Deficiency																				
Studies — Accuracy	Study 1		Study 2		Study 3		Study 4		Study 5		Study 6		Study 7		Study 8		Study 9		Study 10	
Speed	Study 1		Study 2		Study 3		Study 4		Study 5		Study 6		Study 7		Study 8		Study 9		Study 10	

MINIMUM 1-MINUTE SPEEDS FOR DIAGNOSTIC TESTS

Sentence No.	Feature	5-Minute Timed Writing Speed – GWAM*																
		20	25	30	35	40	45	50	55	60	65	70	75	80	85	90	95	100
1	Simple vocabulary	26	31	36	41	46	52	59	66	74	81	88	93	98	103	108	113	118
2	High-stroke intensity	22	27	32	36	41	46	52	60	67	73	78	83	88	93	98	103	108
3	Alternate hands	26	31	36	41	46	51	56	62	68	74	80	86	92	97	102	107	112
4	Compound strokes	24	29	35	40	46	52	58	64	70	76	82	88	94	99	104	109	114
5	Vertical strokes	18	23	28	33	38	43	48	53	58	62	66	70	74	78	82	86	90
6	Double letters	20	25	30	35	40	47	54	58	62	66	70	73	76	82	87	92	97
7	One-hand words	18	23	28	33	38	44	51	55	60	64	68	71	74	80	85	90	95
8	Alphabetic	20	25	30	35	40	47	54	59	64	69	74	77	80	84	89	94	99
9	Frequent spacing	28	33	38	43	48	54	60	67	74	79	84	90	96	101	106	111	116
10	Frequent shifting	10	14	18	22	28	34	40	45	50	55	59	63	67	71	76	80	84

*Refer to Chart 1 for your GWAM speed on your first 5-minute timed writing, and round off your speed to the nearest 5.

Drill 9

Listening to interesting neighbors is a wonderful way to enlarge your mind.
Ancient mariners would heed the guiding lighthouses on their homeward trek.
Everything important relating to your theory is awaiting our corroboration.
Their beautiful forefathers worshiped faithfully despite their adversities.
A knowledge of credit is desirable to alleviate serious financial problems.

Drill 10

My country is in a precarious financial condition that necessitates action.
Their authority is concerned about maintaining excellent quality standards.
Everyone concluded that removing the chastised neighbor would be temporary.
Excellent progress in typing depends on quality skill-development programs.
Sundry individuals readily relate to others in similar positions of wealth.

Speed and Accuracy Analysis

Chart 3 on page 16 records the speed and number of errors made on each Diagnostic Test sentence, identifies weaknesses in accuracy and speed, and prescribes corrective practice on the Accuracy Studies.

For each sentence, and in the appropriate Pretest or Posttest column:

1. Compute the gross words a minute (GWAM) speed. Each line has 14 words. Multiply by 14, the number of complete lines. Add the number of additional words from the incomplete line by using the scale at the bottom of the timing.

2. Determine your accuracy. Count the errors and enter that number in the upper part of the "Errors" box. Circle that number if it is 4 or more.

3. Compute the correct words a minute (CWAM) speed: GWAM speed minus 1 word (or point) for each error. Round off the result, if necessary. Enter this number in the CWAM box.

4. Determine the minimum speed:
   a. From Chart 1, note your GWAM speed on your first 5-Minute Timed Writing. Round off your speed to the nearest 5. Use this number to determine the minimum speed for each sentence.
   b. In the "Minimum 1-Minute Speed" table at the bottom of Chart 3, locate the number of the sentence you are working on, and follow it across to the column that reflects the GWAM speed you just determined. The number in this column is the minimum speed for that sentence.
   c. Enter the minimum speed in the "Minimum" box.

5. Determine your speed deficiency. Compare your CWAM speed with the minimum speed. If your CWAM speed is less than the minimum, record the difference between the two speeds in the upper half of the "Deficiency" box. If your CWAM speed is higher than the minimum, leave the "Deficiency" box blank.

6. Prioritize corrective practice for *accuracy*. Corrective practice for accuracy is determined from the "Errors" boxes, and the drills prescribed will be drills from the Accuracy Studies given at the bottom of the chart.

   For boxes with 4 or more errors, sequence the errors from highest to lowest, and enter the sequence numbers in the bottom half of those "Errors" boxes. The numbers indicate the order in which you will do the drills assigned for corrective practice. Begin your corrective practice on the sentence that had the highest number of errors, followed by the sentence that had the second highest number of errors, then the sentence with the third highest number of errors, and so on.

7. Prioritize corrective practice for *speed*. Corrective practice for speed is determined from the "Deficiency" boxes, and the drills prescribed will be drills from the Speed Studies given at the bottom of the chart.

   For the boxes containing a deficiency, sequence the deficiencies from highest to lowest, and enter the sequence numbers in the bottom half of those "Deficiency" boxes. The numbers indicate the order in which you will do the drills assigned for corrective practice. Begin your corrective practice on the sentence that had the highest number of deficiencies, followed by the sentence that had the second highest number of deficiencies, then the sentence with the third highest number of deficiencies, and so on.

Drill 4

A famous woman furnished them with somewhat practical information.
The element of competition constitutes a serious spending problem.
A combination of amusing anecdotes provided the proper atmosphere.
The influential instructor contemplated a flexible typing program.
It is somewhat comforting to achieve fantastic progress in typing.

Drill 5

Hostile conditions on the peninsula dissuaded us from the adventure.
The intelligent deployment of strategic weaponry is a major concern.
You must endeavor to determine your chosen fields of specialization.
Separating families encourages the destruction of family solidarity.
Modern methods are available so you can achieve tremendous progress.

Drill 6

You will eventually comprehend how you developed your speed in typing.
Your vivid imagination makes an important contribution to the picture.
A naturalist was particularly concerned about substantial differences.
A sojourn on the highway provided us a pleasant respite from drudgery.
An improvement in clerical skills represents a helpful accomplishment.

Drill 7

Mastering the "art" of typing requires the application of motion studies.
Satisfaction is a pleasant personal experience derived from achievements.
Maintaining the character of a restaurant augments the proper atmosphere.
Your author's judgment in handling the disciplinary problem is erroneous.
Our traditional caloric indulgence at holiday time is a national problem.

Drill 8

You can make outstanding progress by watching and listening to champions.
The gracious hospitality of the inhabitants enhanced the marvelous party.
A generation of companionship provided us insight into amiable relations.
Further significant information may conflict with our fundamental belief.
Specialized courtesy programs will enable our country to undergo changes.

MINIMUM 1-MINUTE SPEEDS FOR DIAGNOSTIC TESTS

Sen-tence No.	Feature	5-Minute Timed Writing Speed – GWAM*																
		20	25	30	35	40	45	50	55	60	65	70	75	80	85	90	95	100
1	Simple vocabulary	26	31	36	41	46	52	59	66	74	81	88	93	98	103	108	113	118
2	High-stroke intensity	22	27	32	36	41	46	52	60	67	73	78	83	88	93	98	103	108
3	Alternate hands	26	31	36	41	46	51	56	62	68	74	80	86	92	97	102	107	112
4	Compound strokes	24	29	35	40	46	52	58	64	70	76	82	88	94	99	104	109	114
5	Vertical strokes	18	23	28	33	38	43	48	53	58	62	66	70	74	78	82	86	90
6	Double letters	20	25	30	35	40	47	54	58	62	66	70	73	76	82	87	92	97
7	One-hand words	18	23	28	33	38	44	51	55	60	64	68	71	74	80	85	90	95
8	Alphabetic	20	25	30	35	40	47	54	59	64	69	74	77	80	84	89	94	99
9	Frequent spacing	28	33	38	43	48	54	60	67	74	79	84	90	96	101	106	111	116
10	Frequent shifting	10	14	18	22	28	34	40	45	50	55	59	63	67	71	76	80	84

*Refer to Chart 1 for your GWAM speed on your first 5-minute timed writing, and round off your speed to the nearest 5.

Figure 8a. Example of "Minimum 1-Minute Speeds" table for Chart 3

	ITEM	Sentence 1		Sentence 2		Sentence 3		Sentence 4		Sentence 5		Sentence 6		Sentence 7		Sentence 8		Sentence 9		Sentence 10	
		PRE	POST	PRE	POST	PRE	POST	PRE	POST	PRE	POST	PRE	POST	PRE	POST	PRE	POST	PRE	POST	PRE	POST
Diagnostic Test 1	Errors	4/2		5/1		3															
	Minimum	46		41		46															
	CWAM	43		45		42															
	Deficiency	3/2		—		4/1															
Diagnostic Test 2	Errors																				
	Minimum																				
	CWAM																				
	Deficiency																				

Figure 8b. Example of completed Chart 3

Speed Study 2

High-Stroke-Intensity Sentences

KEY FOR DUPLICATION, NOT CONCENTRATION

Goal: To develop fluency in typing long words.

Features: Each sentence contains a large number of long words. These sentences are arranged so that those with the smallest number of long words precede those that have a heavier concentration of them in each drill.

Line: 75 spaces, longest

Drill Assignment: These assignments are for both Pretest/Posttest and Supplemental Diagnostic Tests. For Diagnostic Test 1, use both Drill 1 and Drill 6; for Diagnostic Test 2, use both Drill 2 and Drill 7; for Diagnostic Test 3, use both Drill 3 and Drill 8; for Diagnostic Test 4, use both Drill 4 and Drill 9; and for Diagnostic Test 5, use both Drill 5 and Drill 10.

Directions: Type each line perfectly five times—not necessarily in succession, but in total. Double-space between groups of five perfect lines. Start typing each sentence slowly, and gradually increase your typing rate as your fingers get accustomed to the sentence.

Drill 1

Their personality and proficiency contributed to their cause.

There is a tendency for our pursuits to thwart our ambitions.

During my college days everything was completely fascinating.

A mysterious element yielded a surprisingly visible vitality.

Something obviously affected their expert financial judgment.

Drill 2

The development of our community would fail without management.

A satisfied customer is another valuable asset of our new firm.

Your personal habits will seldom be very interesting to others.

Whatever originates at the gathering may vindicate our beliefs.

Important achievement is possible if tremendous effort is made.

Drill 3

Everyone questioned antisocial behavior and found it undesirable.

A dynamic, economical program of the institution is an advantage.

He is an ardent individual and a very qualified attention getter.

The youngster's predilection for mischief tempers our generosity.

Amiable customers eliminate problems confronting many businesses.

Chart 4: Record of Skill-Development Paragraphs

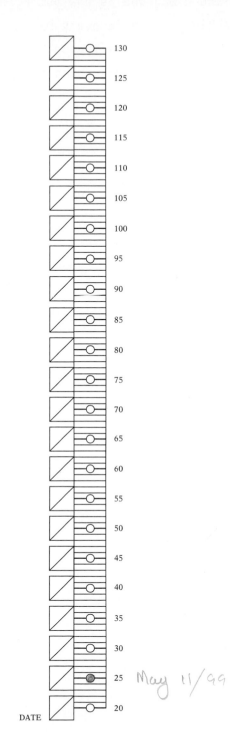

DATE

May 11/99

1. Begin with the 20-WAM Skill-Development Paragraph.
2. Fill in the circle of each paragraph that you key in 1 minute with zero errors.
3. Fill in the corresponding "Date" box with the month and day the paragraph was successfully completed.

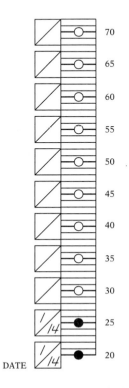

Figure 9. Example of Chart 4

Drill 9

Do we wish to go to the hot jail to find a man who is now out of his mind?
Do all the good you can to all the people you can in every manner you can.
If they work hard at their typing, they should be very good at their work.
Whether or not we wish to turn down the option is something to be decided.
An extra practice period each day will help you improve your typing speed.

Drill 10

It is time for the boy and man to fish in the stream to catch their dinner.
You will be a good typist if you will follow the paths of typing champions.
It is better to have tried typing once and failed than never to have tried.
Do your best in typing daily and you will be very pleased with the results.
After doing these drills, your typing rate should be tremendously improved.

Section
Three

**DO NOT LOOK
AT YOUR
KEYBOARD**

Championship
Warmup Drills

Goal: To develop fluency in keying various stroke combinations.

Features: These drills contain a systematic arrangement of basic stroke combinations that are readily applicable to high-speed development in typing.

Line: 75 spaces

Word Wrap: OFF

Directions: Key these Warmup Drills the first 5 minutes of each day. Key each drill line 1 time. Double-space after each drill. Key as many drills as you can in 5 minutes. Repeat the sequence if you have time.

Drill 4

Now and then it is true that we can do very well if we want to do so.
This is the time for men and women to come to the aid of their party.
If your ship sails due north, it will come near the top of the world.
A good personality will make it easier for them to make good friends.
To make the best progress, therefore, do your best work at all times.

Drill 5

See if I can go and help them to do a fine job for the men and women.
Now is a fine time to do some of the great things you may want to do.
You should give your employers the best you have or seek another job.
It is a fact that the faster you type the more you will like to type.
There are some folks who will go to the south to find what they want.

Drill 6

Is it for the lack of faith and work that we fail in a task hard to do?
I am sorry that you are not sure of the two women who came to our home.
His day has come and so will yours if you try to do your best each day.
He and they should go to their jobs today if it does not rain too much.
She may not put the effort into typing that she must do to become fast.

Drill 7

On a hot day the girl went for a walk to see the big rocks with her dad.
The ten men ran down the lane, and it is up to the judges as to who won.
It will be a fine thing if we do what is paid for or refund their money.
During our time of need, we may go to our friends for help and sympathy.
One thing is certain--good practice will produce good results in typing.

Drill 8

It is a fact that more and more fine jobs will go to the fastest typists.
Knowing what to type and how to type is the fastest way to make progress.
It is the souls of men and women which permit them to rise above animals.
One can endure many trials, but the lack of progress is one of the worst.
Try to strike your keys in a steady, timely fashion without undue pauses.

Drill 1

Second Row (Home Row)

```
a;sldkfjghfjdksla;sldkfjghfjdksla;sldkfjghfjdksla;sldkfjghfjdksla;
```

Drill 2

Second and Third Rows

```
a;qpslwodkeifjrughtyfjrudkeislwoa;qpslwodkeifjrughtyfjrudkeislwoa;qp
```

Drill 3

Second and First Rows

```
a;z/slx.dkc,fjvmghbnfjvmdkc,slx.a;z/slx.dkc,fjvmghbnfjvmdkc,slx.a;z/
```

Drill 4

Second, Third, and First Rows

```
a;qpa;z/slwoslx.dkeidkc,fjrufjvmghtyghbnfjrufjvmdkeidkc,slwoslx.a;qpa;z/
```

Drill 5

Second and Third Rows

```
aq;pswlodekifrjugthyfrjudekiswloaq;pswlodekifrjugthyfrjudekiswloaq;p
```

Drill 6

Second and First Rows

```
az;/sxl.dck,fvjmgbhnfvjmdck,sxl.az;/sxl.dck,fvjmgbhnfvjmdck,sxl.az;/
```

Drill 7

Third and Second Rows

```
qap;wsoledikrfujtgyhrfujedikwsolqap;wsoledikrfujtgyhrfujedikwsolqap;
```

Speed Study 1

Simple-Vocabulary Sentences

SIT BACK IN YOUR CHAIR

Goal: To develop fluency in typing common, simple words.

Features: These sentences contain a concentration of the 200 most commonly used words in the English language.

Line: 75 spaces, longest

Drill Assignment: These assignments are for both Pretest/Posttest and Supplemental Diagnostic Tests. For Diagnostic Test 1, use both Drill 1 and Drill 6; for Diagnostic Test 2, use both Drill 2 and Drill 7; for Diagnostic Test 3, use both Drill 3 and Drill 8; for Diagnostic Test 4, use both Drill 4 and Drill 9; and for Diagnostic Test 5, use both Drill 5 and Drill 10.

Directions: Type each line perfectly five times, not necessarily in succession, but in total. If you make an error in typing a line, begin a new line. Double-space between groups of five perfect lines. Begin at a slow rate of speed, and gradually increase your typing rate until you are typing at a fast, accurate rate of speed.

Drill 1

```
You must force yourself to type fast, so make an effort to do so.

It is up to you and me to find out if he is to go to the pit now.

Our boy is to go to the file and do some work on it at this time.

Six men will come to the aid of the boys and girls of this store.

More and more men and women will vote this year in the elections.
```

Drill 2

```
If we like to type, we will do it as well as it is in us to do so.

It is not what you do, but the way you do it that counts the most.

If the fox can run faster than the dog, it will get away this day.

Now it is up to you to type fast and without errors when you type.

To see a champion typist at work is like viewing poetry in motion.
```

Drill 3

```
In a day or two I may turn down the quiet man from the nearby city.

The past day is one we will find more and more to our satisfaction.

Typing a simple sentence, many times, is a good way to build speed.

It does not matter whether you type fast or slow; type with rhythm.

You will improve your typing if you will practice the right things.
```

Section Four

5-Minute Timed Writings

Goal: To develop speed and accuracy in typing ordinary straight copy for a period of 5 minutes.

Features: Much of the subject matter pertains to the championship background of the author, and the copy contains an appropriate mixture of stroke patterns.

Line: 75 spaces

Word Wrap: ON

Directions: Try not to exceed 5 errors on any 5-Minute Timed Writing. Record the results on Charts 1 and 2, following the directions on the charts. If you take two attempts on the same 5-Minute Timed Writing, record the results of only the better of the two attempts. **Honor Roll Papers:** If you key a 5-Minute Timed Writing with 0 to 1 error and match the NWAM speed of your most recent timed writing, you have keyed a *Speed Honor Roll Paper.* If you key a 5-Minute Timed Writing with 0 to 1 error and come within 3 NWAM of the speed of your most recent timed writing, then you have keyed an *Accuracy Honor Roll Paper.* If you key a 5-Minute Timed Writing with 0 to 1 error and exceed your most recent timed writing by 5 NWAM, you have keyed a *Super Honor Roll Paper.*

Speed Studies

Goal: To provide practice on drills specially constructed to promote speed.

Features: These Speed Studies are constructed to emphasize particular stroke combinations.

1. Simple-Vocabulary Sentences
2. High-Stroke-Intensity Sentences
3. Alternate-Hand Sentences
4. Compound- and Multiple-Stroke Sentences
5. Vertical-Stroke Sentences
6. Double-Letter Sentences
7. One-Hand-Word Sentences
8. Alphabetic Sentences
9. Frequent-Spacing Sentences
10. Frequent-Shifting Sentences

Line: Varies

Word Wrap: OFF

Directions: Follow the directions for each study.

I know you are curious about how championship typing was acquired by 14
my family, and it is a very interesting story which I will be delighted to 29
share with you. My paternal grandfather was a watchmaker. One day a man 44
brought his watch in for repairs. A week later he came to reclaim his 58
watch, but he did not have sufficient funds to pay for it. However, he had 73
a typewriter and offered to exchange his typewriter for his watch. In 87
those days, bartering was a common practice, so my grandfather agreed to 102
the exchange. 105

At that time my father was eleven years old and began tinkering with 119
the typewriter. Then, he began pecking out his lessons, using only two or 134
three fingers. His mother, noticing his fascination with the typewriter, 149
purchased a typing book for him so he could learn to use all of his fingers 164
in a systematic manner. My father then taught himself how to type. He 178
became so fluent in his typing that his typing teacher was amazed. At the 193
age of fifteen, my father could type at the rate of eighty net words a 207
minute on a ten-minute timing. Not satisfied with typing only eighty words 223
a minute, my father approached his teacher as to what he could do to 236
increase his speed to one hundred words a minute. His teacher, not knowing 252
anything about championship typing techniques and methods, told my father 266
to practice three hours every day for an entire year, which meant that my 281
father practiced more than one thousand hours. 291

My father was overjoyed at the prospect of being able to type one 304
hundred words a minute at the age of sixteen. He could hardly wait to get 319
home and begin practicing. My father did not want to take the chance of 334
being one or two words short of his goal, so since he did not have to 348
attend school on Saturdays, he decided that instead of practicing three 362
hours he would practice four or five. According to my father, he practiced 377
assiduously, and it was the longest year of his life. Finally, the year 392
ended, and he rushed to school to take a ten-minute timing. Much to his 406
amazement and disgust, he typed exactly eighty net words a minute. Despite 422
practicing a great deal more than a thousand hours, he had not gained a 436
single word in speed. I am certain you can imagine how he felt. He had 451
wasted a year of his life, all for nothing! 459

Fortunately for my father, the world champion typist came to my 472
father's high school. You can imagine who the first student was to greet 487
the champion! 490

| 1 | 2 | 3 | 4 | 5 | 6 | 7 | 8 | 9 | 10 | 11 | 12 | 13 | 14 | 15 |

Drill 3

.stluser derised eht eveihca dluow taht od dluoc I tahw derednow I
.eulb eht fo tuo tlob a ekil em ot emac ti ekawa-flah yal I sa thgin enO
-pyt rieht no yletelpmoc etartnecnoc stneduts ym ekam ot yaw tseb ehT
,esruoc fo ,tnaem sihT .sdrawkcab epyt yeht taht eriuqer ot eb dluow gni
.ylgnidrocca epyt dna tfel ot thgir morf daer ot dah stneduts eht taht
a teg ton did I taht yrros erew yeht em dlot stneduts ynam ,emit taht tA
ot hcaorppa levon siht gnizilautpecnoc fo daetsni ,peels s'thgin lluf
sraey ytriht naht erom ,yadoT .srorre noitartnecnoc rieht gniyfitcer
gnitcerroc ot troser lanif a sa sdrawkcab gnipyt gnisu llits ma I ,retal
.tneduts elgnis yreve no gnikrow llits si ti dna ,srorre noitartnecnoc

Drill 4

ynam nees evah I ,moorssalc gnipyt eht ni neeb evah I sraey eht revO
ti ,sesac emos ni dna ,ylreporp gnitartnecnoc ytluciffid dah ohw stneduts
yreve ni ,revewoH .laicifeneb ton saw sdrawkcab gnipyt taht deraeppa sah
yletelpmoc gnitartnecnoc smelborp dah ohw stneduts eht fo lla ,ssalc elgnis
-kcab gnipyt yb devloser ylirotcafsitas melborp eht dah gnipyt rieht no
;sdrawkcab sllird wef a gnipyt deriuqer ylno ti ,secnatsni emos nI .sdraw
;sdrawkcab depyt eb ot dah sllird fo tes eritne eht ,sesac emos ni elihw
.semit eerht ro owt sllird fo tes eritne eht epyt ot dah srehto wef a dna
-woh ;yrogetac hcae otni llaf lliw ohw enimretederp ot elbissop ton si tI
ot tnemngissa siht fo sgnipyt eerht ro ,owt ,eno sekat ti rehtehw ,reve
latnem yrassecen eht deriuqca evah uoy taht si gniht tnatropmi eht ,eciffus
.ti htrow eb ylniatrec lliw tI .tsipyt etarucca na emoceb ot enilpicsid

Drill 5

eht epyt ot evah lliw ohw stneduts eht fo eno eb ot neppah uoy fI
elbuod uoy taht tseggus dluow I ,ecno naht erom tnemngissa sdrawkcab gnipyt
,sdrow rehto nI .epyt lliw uoy taht hcae fo senil tcefrep fo rebmun eht
senil tcefrep owt epyt ot dah uoy ,tnemngissa siht depyt uoy emit tsrif eht
fo rebmun eht elbuod ,tnemngissa siht epyt uoy emit dnoces ehT .hcae fo
-nigeb ,hcae fo senil tcefrep ruof epyt lliw uoy os ,hcae fo senil tcefrep
dah evah I .yrassecen fi ,62 ydutS hguorht epyt dna 32 ydutS htiw gnin
driht a tnemngissa eht epyt ot dah ohw dnasuoht net fo tuo tneduts eno ylno
setunim evif epyt ot elba saw ehs ,ti gnipyt detelpmoc ehs nehw dna ,emit
-woh ,emit taht ot roirP .rorre eno naht erom on htiw ypoc thgiarts morf
.gnimit etunim-evif a no srorre ytriht ot neetfif morf ekam dluow ehs ,reve
.gnipyt ni noitartnecnoc latot fo ecnatropmi eht setacidni ylraelc sihT

Words

The world champion at that time was George Hossfield. My father told | 14
his sad story of practicing for more than a thousand hours without gaining | 29
a single word. The champion felt sorry for my father and asked him to sit | 44
at his typewriter so he could ascertain what my father was doing | 57
incorrectly. You can imagine how excited my dad was because he was going | 72
to have his techniques critiqued by the world typewriting champion. | 86

My father's heart was palpitating, his hands were sweating, and his | 99
breathing rate accelerated as he sat down at the champion's typewriter. My | 115
father started typing, as fast as he could, eighty words a minute. He had | 130
just completed about two-and-a-half lines when the champion told him to | 144
stop. My father wanted to know what was wrong. The champion began to | 158
itemize all of the incorrect techniques he had observed. My father was | 173
dumbfounded because he was doing everything his high school teacher had | 187
taught him. Furthermore, he had read every typewriting book at the Library | 202
of Congress so he would not waste time doing things incorrectly. | 215

The champion sat at the typewriter and typed for a minute so my father | 230
could see the difference between the techniques he was taught and the | 244
techniques used by the world typewriting champion. The difference was | 258
amazing. My father could readily understand why he had not made any | 272
progress in typing despite the fact that he had practiced for more than one | 287
thousand hours. Practice in and of itself will not make you an excellent | 302
typist; it is perfect practice that makes perfect. | 312

After my dad saw the imperfections in his typing techniques, he began | 326
to wonder if it were still possible for him to realize his dream of typing | 341
one hundred words a minute. He still had two intricate problems: how many | 356
hours a day he should practice and what he should practice. Therefore, he | 371
asked the champion exactly what he should do in order to realize his goal | 386
of typing one hundred words a minute. | 394

The champion suggested that he continue to practice his typing three | 408
hours every day and outlined exactly what he should practice. Meeting the | 423
champion provided my father with a great deal of motivation, and he | 436
practiced his typing with plenty of zest and enthusiasm. My father | 450
immediately noticed an improvement in his speed. I have found that | 463
practicing the right thing, the right way, and with the right attitude is | 478
sure to produce positive results. | 485

| 1 | 2 | 3 | 4 | 5 | 6 | 7 | 8 | 9 | 10 | 11 | 12 | 13 | 14 | 15 |

Accuracy Study 27

Intensive Concentration Drills— Reverse Typing

Goal: To require intensive concentration, thereby facilitating the acquisition of the mental discipline necessary for accurate typing.

Features: These drills are shown typed backward to compel you to concentrate totally on each letter in each word and will easily be readable when typed correctly.

Line: 75 spaces

Directions: Type each paragraph on a line-for-line basis, reading from right to left. Type each line perfectly three times. When you make an error, begin a new line immediately and type that line until you type it perfectly. When you complete a line, the typing will be in the normal sequence of reading. Therefore, you will not encounter any difficulty reading what you have typed. Double-space between each drill and each set of three perfect lines. Type slowly and spell each word out—spelling and typing simultaneously.

Drill 1

```
gniriuqca si gnitirwepyt fo lla ni smelborp tluciffid tsom eht fo enO
   slaudividni weF  .tsipyt etarucca yrev a emoceb ot enilpicsid latnem eht
      ot deriuqer noitartnecnoc etulosba dna latot eht fo noitpecnoc yna evah
         poleved tsum uoy taht uoy erussa em teL  .yletarucca ylbanosaer epyt
-ni emos nI  .yletarucca epyt ot redro ni srewop evitartnecnoc suodnemert
   sdrawkcab tnemngissa na epyt ot tneduts a rof yrassecen si ti ,secnats
   si sihT  .gnipyt reh ro sih no etartnecnoc ot elba si tneduts eht erofeb
      .tnasaelp yrev ton si ti wonk I dna ,tnemom siht ta gniod era uoy tahw
I ,gnipyt fo esahp siht retsam ot evirts ot eunitnoc ylno lliw uoy fi ,teY
         .eveihca lliw uoy stluser eht htiw desaelp yrev eb lliw uoy wonk
```

Drill 2

```
   I--oga sraey ytriht naht erom--gnipyt gnihcaet nageb tsrif I nehW
   -of ytluciffid fo laed taerg a dah ohw stneduts fo rebmun a deretnuocne
rehtie dluow yehT  .gnipyt erew yeht tahw no noitnetta eritne rieht gnisuc
kniht dluow yeht ro gnipyt erew yeht tahw fo txetnoc eht ni detseretni teg
-ert a edam stneduts ynam ,ecneuqesnoc a sA  .rettam suoenartxe emos tuoba
   gnittimo ,srettel gnidda sa hcus ,srorre noitartnecnoc fo rebmun suodnem
ylraelc sihT  .srettel gnorw eht gnilbuod ro ,srettel gnisopsnart ,srettel
   enilpicsid latnem reporp eht depoleved ton dah yeht taht em ot detacidni
-inam noitartnecnoc fo kcal eht yb delbuort os saw I  .yletarucca epyt ot
      .detnemelpmi eb ot dah serusaem citsard emos wenk I taht detsef
```

Words

A great deal has been written about champions in many fields, but 13
little has been written about champion typists. Since this book is about 28
championship typing techniques and methods, the characteristics found in 43
the rarest of all champions, the champion typist, will be considered. 57

It is an electrifying, motivating experience to watch a champion's 70
fingers flying over the keyboard at more than one hundred and sixty words a 86
minute without making a single error. There is nothing more dramatic to a 101
student than to observe a champion typist in action. 111

Champion typists are made; they are not born. However, there are some 126
indispensable qualities cultivated in a champion that distinguish that 140
individual from ordinary typists. There is a subtle combination of 153
ability, perception, perseverance, and dedication within the individual 168
that is augmented by the long, sometimes frustrating, and often tedious 182
hours, weeks, and even years of practice needed to reach the final goal. 197

The champion soon learns that technique is the major concern. What 211
may appear insignificant to an ordinary typist is of paramount importance 225
to a champion. The height of the chair or desk is a tremendous factor, 240
since one inch can make the difference of at least ten net words a minute. 255
A quick, firm striking of the keys is essential for speed. Fingers should 270
never linger on the keys, and fingers should be curved and hover close to 285
the keyboard. Incorrect stroking will result in errors and loss of speed. 300

So many different reaches are involved in typing that one must master 314
each one of them to avoid jerky motions or unnecessary pauses and to 328
develop smoothness and continuity in stroking. 337

Just as champions learned from laborious practice, you, too, must 351
first learn how to work with your machine if you wish to develop superior 365
typing skills. Striking the keys correctly is a technique which must be 380
developed before you can reach a high level of speed and accuracy. There 395
are several critical areas you should emphasize: position of the fingers, 410
wrists, forearms, and elbows; touch; rhythm; and total concentration. 424

Although you may spend your working day with fingers flying over a 437
keyboard, there are probably some mistakes you continue to make. These 452
problems must be attacked separately by analyzing each area and practicing 467
until the difficulty is eliminated. There is no substitute for proper 481
practice methods and techniques, so learn the championship way and start on 496
the road to high-speed typing. 502

| 1 | 2 | 3 | 4 | 5 | 6 | 7 | 8 | 9 | 10 | 11 | 12 | 13 | 14 | 15 |

Accuracy Study 26

Concentration Drills—Split Doublets

ARMS AND WRISTS STEADY

Goal: To increase accuracy by improving concentration, thereby facilitating the typing of split doublets (in which one word ends and the next word begins with the same letter).

Features: These drills consist of phrases containing split doublets, which constitute a major typing problem to anyone typing at a high rate of speed. These drills will require a high degree of concentration in order to avoid omitting the second half of the doublet.

Line: 75 spaces

Directions: Type each line perfectly three times—not necessarily in succession, but in total. Begin a new line immediately when you make an error. Double-space between groups of three perfect lines. In order to type split doublets accurately, it may be necessary for you to spell out each letter. Begin typing each line slowly, and gradually increase your typing rate.

Drill 1

```
the civic center the civic center the civic center the civic center
and the red dogs and the red dogs and the red dogs and the red dogs
and the big gate and the big gate and the big gate and the big gate
and high-handed and high-handed and high-handed and high-handed and
```

Drill 2

```
and on notice and on notice and on notice and on notice and on notice
and the error and the error and the error and the error and the error
left or right left or right left or right left or right left or right
and jab badly and jab badly and jab badly and jab badly and jab badly
```

Drill 3

```
and is sure and is sure and is sure and is sure and is sure and is sure
and top pay and top pay and top pay and top pay and top pay and top pay
and after reading and after reading and after reading and after reading
and will look kindly and will look kindly and will look kindly and will
```

Drill 4

```
know why and know why and know why and know why and know why and know why
so often and so often and so often and so often and so often and so often
my youth and my youth and my youth and my youth and my youth and my youth
if found and if found and if found and if found and if found and if found
```

Drill 5

```
in nothing flat in nothing flat in nothing flat in nothing flat in nothing
the quick kill the quick kill the quick kill the quick kill the quick kill
they saw women they saw women they saw women they saw women they saw women
and that thing and that thing and that thing and that thing and that thing
```

Words

When the typewriter was invented, the manufacturers held typewriting 14
contests to prove that a person could type faster than he could write. 28
Four months after my father had met George Hossfield and learned 41
championship typing techniques, he became the first high school student in 56
America to win the Platinum Pin for excellence in typing. It had eight 71
diamonds and eight emeralds. To win this award, my father typed fifteen 85
minutes from unfamiliar straight copy at the rate of one hundred words 100
a minute without an error. Had my father not been exposed to world 113
championship typing techniques, I am certain he would have remained an 127
eighty-words-a-minute typist. 133

During the early years of competition, the word count was based on 147
dictionary words. For high speeds to be set, many small words constituted 162
the straight copy. The speeds were somewhat higher than those set in more 177
recent years. In order to have more uniform scoring, a five-stroke word 192
count was introduced. This provides us with a more accurate assessment of 207
speed rates, and this is what we use today in calculating speeds. 220

After winning the Platinum Pin, my father had another goal and that 234
was to win the World's Amateur Typewriting Championship. Therefore, he 248
continued to practice many hours every day and entered the world 261
championship typewriting contest when he was eighteen years old. The 275
contest was held in New York City. All contestants were requested to 289
report a few days before the contest for a trial run, so the officials of 304
the contest could eliminate those who had no chance of winning anything. 318

My father purposely typed about ten words slower than his top speed. 333
Nevertheless, he finished second in the trial. When the contest began, my 348
father was nervously opening and closing the drawers of his desk; he was 362
the last person to begin. Thirty minutes later, my father had set a world 377
typing record for amateur typists. This was the beginning of an 390
illustrious typing career. 396

Over fifty years ago, my father could type faster on the nonelectric 409
typewriter than anyone else in history, and five strokes constituted a word. 425
At the end of sixty minutes of typing from unfamiliar straight copy, he had 440
typed, with ninety-nine percent accuracy, one thousand strokes more than 455
anyone else had ever typed. 460

| 1 | 2 | 3 | 4 | 5 | 6 | 7 | 8 | 9 | 10 | 11 | 12 | 13 | 14 | 15 |

Drill 6

By now, you probably are beginning to acquire the mental discipline you need in order to be able to concentrate completely on your typing--spelling out each word, letter for letter--thereby greatly reducing the number of typing errors you will make on a timed writing. You probably are smiling more as you are beginning to master the art of typing. Your prospects for employment will be greatly enhanced once you develop a high level of skill in typing. You probably no longer dread the thought of having to type. Of even greater importance, you have learned something about yourself--you were able to persevere under the most trying circumstances, and you have now acquired the mental discipline necessary to become a very successful person in typing as well as in other areas.

	Words
In my opinion, the most important aspect of keyboarding with a high	14
degree of speed and accuracy is perfecting your keyboarding techniques.	28
You have noticed that I have emphasized world championship keyboarding	43
techniques over and over again. Without perfecting your techniques, you	57
will not be able to progress at a satisfactory pace. Therefore, heed my	72
advice. I could not have achieved the speed and accuracy skills that I	86
possess without heeding the advice my father gave me when I started	100
learning to type. I am certain the same will be true in your case also.	114
One merely has to reflect on what happened to my father when he was	128
sixteen years old. He spent an entire year practicing more than one	142
thousand hours without gaining a single word. You can imagine how	155
depressing that was for him, and yet he became the fastest typist of all	170
time on a nonelectric typewriter after he was introduced to world	183
championship techniques.	188
High speed in typing is directly related to good typing techniques, so	203
I advise you to constantly review the world championship techniques	216
indicated in this program. I had the advantage of seeing world	229
championship typing techniques practically my entire life, and I knew that	244
if these techniques were good enough for my father to win world	257
championships in typing, they certainly were good enough for me.	270
Of these championship techniques, one of the most important is keying	284
at a smooth pace. This is one of the strategies emphasized by my father to	299
me. I was indeed fortunate to have a world champion as a father and	313
teacher of typing because I did not waste time doing things incorrectly.	328
My father always wanted to write a typing book, but he was too busy.	342
You can imagine what his life was like. He probably demonstrated his	356
typing prowess before more people than anyone ever. I don't know how many	371
people saw his demonstrations on television or in the movies or heard his	386
blazing speed on the radio. My dad was on most of the big television	400
shows, and he motivated tens of millions of individuals.	411
My father always told me that a lifetime was too short, and you never	425
have enough time to do everything you may wish to do. He was correct, so	440
he taught me everything it had taken him a lifetime to learn. This program	455
could not have been written without the knowledge and expertise I received	470
from him.	472

| 1 | 2 | 3 | 4 | 5 | 6 | 7 | 8 | 9 | 10 | 11 | 12 | 13 | 14 | 15 |

Drill 3

Whenever students fail to respond to the preceding assignments, it has generally been true that the ultimate solution to the problem is the most dreadful experience of all--typing backwards. This subjects the student to the most extreme mental pressure, and it also subjects the student to the most trying typing exercise imaginable. Initially, many students get very frustrated. Some become very angry and upset because of the difficulty of typing exactly contrary to the conventional method. Nevertheless, if you will just keep on trying to type backwards, no matter how vexing or frustrating it is, sooner or later you will acquire the mental discipline that is necessary to become a very accurate typist.

Drill 4

To type this paragraph backwards--reading each line of copy from right to left--will require absolute, total, and complete concentration. This kind of concentration is essential if you are to become a highly accurate typist. Many students who made numerous errors prior to completing this assignment became very accurate typists shortly after finishing this drill. It seems as though someone had uttered a magical word. Students are simply amazed at their own transformation as they are able to type both rapidly and accurately. Therefore, it is to your advantage to concentrate intently on typing each stroke in each word, because once you acquire the necessary mental discipline, you will become a highly skilled typist.

Drill 5

While this particular assignment is very demanding, you must persevere and, if possible, laugh at your difficulty in typing backwards. Slowly but surely, you will be acquiring better concentration, and as you do, you will find that the number of mental errors you make will decrease until, much to your surprise, you will be making very few concentration errors. The best way for you to eliminate concentration errors is by spelling out each word, typing letter for letter. In typing backwards, you are compelled to spell out each word, as it is the only way you can type this assignment with complete accuracy. It may seem to you to be nonsensical to type backwards, but it will be very beneficial, believe me.

	Words
Developing skill in typing builds character because typing uses a	13
mixture of pliability, perseverance, discipline, and honesty to achieve	28
this important motor skill. You must develop all these characteristics if	43
you wish to master and excel in typing. It also takes a great deal of	57
human intelligence and human will to apply the basic mechanics. Typing is	72
not an easy skill, and to achieve success, you must set realistic goals.	87
You may, after an honest self-analysis, be compelled to admit that your	101
goals need to be redefined.	107
You must educate yourself both in class and out of class. Typing	120
skill is not free. It is not something you receive or have presented to	135
you as a gift. The only way in which you can obtain it is to want it	149
enough to pay for it with your own efforts. You must earn this skill, just	164
as you must earn everything else that is really valuable to you.	177
You, more than anyone else, determine how fast you will acquire typing	191
proficiency. No matter how much and how well you are taught, no matter	206
what opportunities you have for learning, you will gain almost nothing	220
unless you take an active interest in remedying your deficiencies. These	235
timed writings will reveal your strong points and your weak points and will	250
emphasize what you need to practice to gain proficiency.	261
A real desire to learn serves as a "self-start." It will give you a	275
driving purpose toward a definite goal. It will keep your mind wide awake	290
and make practice interesting, and even exciting. Without waiting to be	305
taught, you should make every effort to attain mastery of this important	320
skill. If, in addition to wanting to learn, you have gained skill in	334
managing yourself and your time and in disciplining your mind, you will	348
make very rapid progress.	353
Unfortunately, some students lack skill in typing because they have	367
not trained themselves to study efficiently. You cannot plod rather	381
blindly through crucial typing assignments day after day and hope to make	396
spectacular progress. If you muddle along wasting your time and energy,	410
you will become discouraged. It is imperative that you study the proper	425
skill-development strategies.	431
Frustrations are a part of becoming an expert typist. To attain	444
typing proficiency, your fingers must respond automatically to the impulse	459
of your brain. If you dedicate yourself to a high standard of perfection	474
in your practicing, you will soon be transformed into a superior typist.	488

| 1 | 2 | 3 | 4 | 5 | 6 | 7 | 8 | 9 | 10 | 11 | 12 | 13 | 14 | 15 |

Accuracy Study 25

Intensive Concentration Drills—Paragraphs

KEY LETTER
FOR LETTER

Goal: To provide the most intensive concentration drill possible, so as to provide the mental discipline essential for accurate typing. These drills will expose you to the most mentally demanding exercises you have ever typed, and if you will conscientiously strive to master each drill, you will be a vastly improved typist.

Features: These drills are composed of ordinary words; yet because of the unique way of typing them, these drills will compel you to concentrate more completely on each typed stroke than ever before. Each drill contains pertinent information that may be helpful to you. Read all six drills before typing this assignment.

Line: 75 spaces

Directions: Type each paragraph on a line-for-line basis, reading and typing from right to left. Type each line perfectly three times—not necessarily in succession, but in total. Double-space between groups of three perfect lines. Strive for perfect typing and perfect rhythm. The first line keyed backward will look like this:

```
poleved ot si stneduts gnipyt tsom rof sksat tluciffid tsom eht fo enO
```

Drill 1

One of the most difficult tasks for most typing students is to develop the mental discipline necessary to become an accurate typist. Due to the fact that most typists have not developed their concentrative capabilities, these students continue to make countless errors and usually are not happy typists. Oddly enough, most students who are experiencing great difficulty in keeping their minds on what they are typing do not know what they must do in order to get the mental discipline they need in order to type more accurately. It has been my experience that the number one problem in typing is the lack of total concentration, and the best way to develop total concentration is by spelling out each word as you type.

Drill 2

It is quite easy to find out if you are making errors owing to a lack of concentration. Your error-analysis chart will reveal the fact that you are leaving out letters, adding letters, transposing letters or words, or doubling the wrong letter. These types of errors clearly reveal a somewhat less than total concentration on what you are typing. In order to type accurately, you must be concentrating so intensely that you are completely oblivious to what is going on around you. Also, your concentration must be so thoroughly focused on each word you are typing that you are unable to comprehend what you are typing. You should read the copy for duplication only, not for comprehension.

Words

A positive attitude is one of the greatest assets. Guard it   12
carefully. Progress and success, whether in the classroom, on the job, or   27
at home, are affected to a great extent by it. Your personality also   41
reveals your readiness to assume the responsibilities involved in a job or   56
in social contacts.   60

Examine your inner self critically to ensure that no negative   73
tendencies intrude. If you have a martyr complex and foster feelings of   88
inferiority or if you make excuses for poor work or for too little done,   102
you are rationalizing deficiencies. Other negative traits that drain you   117
of vitality, rob you of efficiency, and dull your brain power are   130
depression, tension, irritation, and intolerance. Your attitude toward   145
your fellow classmates or workers, toward supervision, and toward   158
responsibility is as important as your attitude about yourself.   171

Psychologists tell us that attitude is an enduring structure of   184
beliefs that causes us to behave selectively toward physical objects,   198
events, and behavior. Thus we conclude that a positive mental concept of   212
our ability and worth is extremely important in striving toward a goal.   227
Conversely, it is impossible to progress satisfactorily in work or live a   242
meaningful life if one is filled with negative perceptions.   254

Perception of yourself is a powerful force that influences and guides   268
you. If you perceive yourself as becoming a successful typist, you will   283
see yourself as responsible for your progress, and you will pinpoint what   297
you do, or fail to do, that causes your success or failure. You will   311
reinforce your attainments and correct your errors. You know that you   326
guide your destiny in typing; and since you perceive that you are   339
competent, you will invest your time, energy, and talents in full measure   354
today so you may reap the benefits of a superior typing skill tomorrow.   358

Typing is one of the most important ways of conveying information.   382
You, the typist, will be judged by the quality of the product produced, and   397
your attitude will be displayed by your work.   406

Two of the most important aspects of a positive attitude are interest   420
and desire. If you are interested, you will absorb more information from   435
your surroundings, and you will become aware of opportunities that further   450
your goal. Desire will make you more creative. These attitudes make you   465
search for new opportunities and new approaches to implement ideas. A   479
person with a positive attitude reflects a sense of accomplishment.   493

| 1 | 2 | 3 | 4 | 5 | 6 | 7 | 8 | 9 | 10 | 11 | 12 | 13 | 14 | 15 |

Drill 3   G, H, and I

ganglionic gastritis gastrointestinal geniculocalcarine gestation
glomerulonephritis glossopharyngeal glucocorticoids gonadotrophic

hallucinations haustration headaches hemolysis hypertension hypertrophy
hexamethonium histamines hyperglycemic hyperparathyroidism hypotonicity

idiopathic ileocecal ileum immunizations inotropic insulin interstitial
intercavernous interventricular intrapulmonary isotonic impenetrability

Drill 4   K, L, M, N, and O

karyology keratin keratoconus ketosis ketosteroids kidney klebsiella
lactation lactogenic leukemia lipoproteins lobotomized luteinization

macrocytes macrophages magenstrasse mediastinitis meningitis metabolical
metarteriole monocytes mononucleosis multimolecular myeloblastic measles

neocerebellum neostigmine nephropathic nephrotic neutrophilia nociceptive
oogenesis ophthalmoscope osmosis ossicular osteoblasts ovaries oxyblepsia

Drill 5   P, R, and S

paleocerebellum palpitation panhypopituitarism paranoia parasympathetic
parathyroid peristalsis phagocytosis phenolsulfonphthalein phonasthenia

regurgitation repolarization resuscitations retinotectal retrotracheal
reticulo retinopathy retina respiratory rhytidome retinitis ricinoleic

sacrococcygeus salpingitis schistosomiasis scrupulosity seminiferous
sensation silicosis sinus substances somatotrophin somesthetic spasm

Drill 6   T, U, and V

tachyphylaxis tachypnea tentorium testes tetraethylammonium thalamus
tachyrhythmia thoracic thrombocytopenia thyroglobulin thyrotoxicosis

ulcer ulcerative umbrage unipolarity ureteral urethra urobilinogen
urine uridine urobilinogen urobilins urogastrone urticaria uveitis

vagotomy valvular varicose vasoconstriction vasodilatation vasomotor
vectorcardiogram ventricular ventricose veratridine ventriculography

Words

The proper mental attitude is essential if one wishes to learn to | 13
type. In fact, without the proper attitude, learning this skill will be | 28
difficult and will result in an unnecessarily frustrating experience. | 42

When observing a champion type rapidly and apparently effortlessly, | 56
one might well conclude that typing is a comparatively easy skill to | 70
acquire. Appearances are tremendously deceptive in this respect. Perhaps | 85
you can remember quite vividly the difficulty you had initially in learning | 100
the computer keyboard. One needs only to study the conditions under which | 115
the old masters perfected typing techniques to realize that it is | 128
impossible to achieve success in typing without using the proper techniques | 143
and without dedicated hard work. Histories of successful people--typists | 158
and others--illustrate all too clearly the lessons of patience and the | 172
efforts of years of practice and discipline. | 181

However, typing does not have to be too difficult if you will learn | 195
the right way to practice. In fact, the championship way you are now | 209
studying is indeed the best way and the simplest way to learn to type. | 223
You must realize that typing is a skill with many facets, and in order to | 238
acquire this skill, you must use various and sundry practice procedures. | 253
The proper techniques were developed by the old masters of typing over a | 268
period of many years. These old masters made a very comprehensive study of | 283
the various typing motions and developed the most expeditious way of making | 298
every stroke and motion in typing. You are learning their methods, and if | 313
you will follow instructions precisely, do exactly what you are told, and | 328
type these drills faithfully and conscientiously, your success as an expert | 343
typist is assured. | 347

Another very crucial ingredient is absolute self-confidence. You must | 361
assume that you are going to succeed in order to learn to type. One of the | 376
surest ways to succeed in typing lies in thoroughness. This means that you | 392
must decide that you are going to master typing, that you will practice | 406
exactly as you are instructed, and that you will practice diligently no | 420
matter how difficult it seems or how much time is required. In typing, a | 435
regard for the small things is necessary. If you can overcome small | 449
worries, you will soon override the greater obstacles you encounter. | 463

It is true that some people become successful typists in less time | 476
than others, but in every instance, putting in much hard work and | 490
developing the correct typing techniques guarantee success. | 501

| 1 | 2 | 3 | 4 | 5 | 6 | 7 | 8 | 9 | 10 | 11 | 12 | 13 | 14 | 15 |

Accuracy Study 24

Concentration Drills—Unusual Words

KEY FOR DUPLICATION, NOT COMPREHENSION

Goal: To provide maximum mental discipline, which is absolutely essential for fast, accurate typing. These drills will compel total concentration.

Features: These drills contain a preponderance of scientific and medical terms. This will be one of the most difficult assignments you have typed or will ever type. Yet it is vitally important that you master typing these unusual words, as it will provide you with excellent mental discipline that is essential to good typing. These lines are double-blocked according to each letter of the alphabet.

Line: 75 spaces

Directions: Type each line perfectly three times—not necessarily in succession, but in total. Begin a new line immediately when you make an error. Double-space between groups of three perfect lines. Because these scientific and medical words are exceedingly difficult to type, you must type each line very slowly, spelling each word out—typing letter for letter. Continue to strive for good accuracy, and endeavor to type at a slow, rhythmic rate.

Drill 1   A, B, and C
```
acetylcholine acidophilic acidosis actomyosin adenosine adrenocortical
agglutinogen agranulocytosis albuminoid aleukemic amenorrhea asthmatic

ballistocardiograph basal benign basophilic bathyesthesia bilirubin
bradycardia bronchitis bronchospirometry bulboventricular berberine

carboxymethylcellulose carboxypolypeptidase carcinogenic carcinomatosis
cardiospasm cardiovascular carotenoid cerebrospinal chronaxie cirrhosis
```

Drill 2   D, E, and F
```
decarboxylation decibels defibrillation desmosome desoxycorticosterone
deaminase dehydration diabetes diastolic Dibenamine dihydrotachysterol

edema electrocardiography electroencephalogram electrolyte emphysema
encephalography endocrinology endometriosis erythroblastosis ethmoid

familial fasciculation fibrillation fibula flatulence flocculonodular
fibrinolysin filariasis flavoproteins fluoroscopic follicular femoral
```

Words

Perseverance--the ability to persist despite obstacles,   11
discouragement, frustration, and opposition--is a quality everyone who has   26
learned to type well possesses. Do not become discouraged when you face   41
days when you cannot get your fingers to react as you want them to do.   55
Typing is a skill that presents countless opportunities for errors. A word   71
may be omitted, letters interchanged, spaces skipped, or capitals missed.   86
Somehow, though, if you will remember to economize your arm and body   99
motions, use the tip of each finger to strike the keys, and keep your hands   115
relaxed and your wrists steady and low, you will soon be on your way up the   130
ladder to high-speed typing.   136

Words are used to portray ideas and provide the reader with mental   149
pictures. You will certainly have a feeling of accomplishment when you   164
achieve the ability to think of words and your fingers react automatically   179
and precisely by typing them perfectly and quickly. Just imagine for a   193
moment that you are thinking ideas, and these ideas and thoughts are being   208
immediately transmitted onto your paper as your fingers fly through the   222
air, landing squarely and quickly on the correct keys. This marvelous   237
experience and exhilarating feeling are well worth the many hours spent in   252
acquiring this magnificent skill.   258

To become an accurate, speedy typist is not as difficult as you might   273
imagine. Yet you must persist in applying the proper keyboarding   286
techniques if you do not want to be trapped by poor posture, improper hand   301
position, and incorrect fingering. Much of the strain of typing comes from   316
improper finger motion and hesitation in locating the proper keys. Of   330
equal importance is being able to identify the particular problem you have   345
in speed or accuracy development. The best way to discover these typing   360
areas of weakness is by using the sophisticated diagnostic charts that are   375
a part of championship typing. If you practice the weaknesses revealed,   389
you will make rapid progress because you are concentrating your efforts on   404
only those areas in which you are experiencing difficulty.   416

Another way to regain your typing composure on a topsy-turvy day is to   431
turn to the one-minute paragraphs and practice the first paragraph until   445
you can type it perfectly in one minute. Then type another paragraph until   460
you have perfected it in one minute, then another and another, until you   475
have acquired mastery of the keyboard again. You will be amazed at how   489
this method will enhance your typing ability.   498

| 1 | 2 | 3 | 4 | 5 | 6 | 7 | 8 | 9 | 10 | 11 | 12 | 13 | 14 | 15 |

Drill 5

continuation	controllable	disciplining	authorization	congressional
disregarding	disorganized	refreshingly	decriminalize	irresponsible
enthusiastic	delineations	requirements	informational	grammatically
appreciative	applications	acknowledged	establishment	excessiveness

Drill 6

merchantable	minimization	impressively	magnificently	unconsciously
salesmanship	tranquillity	sophisticate	superlatively	transcription
recalcitrant	perpetrators	constructive	undergraduate	disappearance
compensating	appreciation	chastisement	entertainment	reconsidering

Drill 7

cohabitation	destinations	equalization	interrogating	technological
distribution	transitional	commutations	progressively	realistically
counterpoint	kleptomaniac	pathetically	exceptionally	confrontation
civilization	perseverance	vanquishable	comprehension	inconceivable

Drill 8

secessionist	apprehension	insurrection	unenforceable	abnormalities
constituency	miscalculate	imponderable	personalities	automatically
dramatically	introduction	consultation	disproportion	sensitivities
unreasonable	compartments	inauguration	investigative	compassionate

Drill 9

extrapolated	misinterpret	expectations	transgression	unequivocally
affectionate	neutralizing	encountering	contradictory	manifestation
unparalleled	deficiencies	infrequently	conveniencing	questionnaire
rehabilitate	indignations	intimidating	unfortunately	parliamentary

Drill 10

shortcomings	irresistible	enthusiastic	ambassadorial	inappropriate
persistently	introduction	availability	unfortunately	justification
denomination	performances	considerably	discrepancies	vulnerability
differential	preferential	asphyxiation	justification	philanthropic

Words

One of the worst problems we have in mastering the keyboard is | 13

acquiring the mental discipline of keeping our minds totally on what we are | 28

doing. It is very easy to find our minds wandering. Of course, when that | 43

happens, you will make a tremendous number of misstrokes. At all times | 57

your complete mental focus must be on what you are doing. | 69

Every now and then you will encounter a student who has a tremendous | 83

concentration problem. Marian was just that type of student. She knew | 97

exactly what was going on in front of her and on both sides of her, as well | 113

as everything I was doing. Because she was always unfocused, she made a | 127

high number of misstrokes. I talked with her repeatedly about her problem, | 142

but she could not break herself of being curious about everything going on | 157

in the room. | 160

Finally, I placed Marian in the first row, right corner of the | 173

classroom, so there would not be anything to catch her eye and attention. | 188

I also made her key on a letter-for-letter basis. It was not long before | 203

Marian was keying for five minutes without a misstroke. Fortunately, most | 218

people do not have Marian's problem, but if you do, talk the matter over | 232

with your teacher. He or she will help you with a keyboarding problem. | 247

Another problem that most students have is looking at their fingers | 260

while they key. This is one of the worst things a student can do. I have | 275

seen many students endeavor to type that way, and all of them have been | 290

unsuccessful in developing a good keyboarding skill. | 300

If you expect to become proficient at typing, then it is essential | 314

that you learn to type using the touch system. If you are not confident of | 329

where certain keys are located, I urge you to review the keyboard. In some | 344

situations, you might have to place a plain sheet of paper on the top of | 359

the keyboard. You would then place your fingers under the paper and on the | 374

guide keys. You would then key for one week with the keys covered. | 388

Usually, after one week of keying in this fashion--and after doing the | 402

necessary corrective practice drills--you will no longer have that problem. | 418

If you have a security problem in locating some of the keys, ask your | 432

teacher to cover your keyboard, assign you the alphabetic sentences to key, | 447

chart your misstrokes, and assign you the appropriate drills to eliminate | 462

that problem. It will take only one week to correct that problem if you | 476

practice conscientiously. | 481

| 1 | 2 | 3 | 4 | 5 | 6 | 7 | 8 | 9 | 10 | 11 | 12 | 13 | 14 | 15

Accuracy Study 23

Concentration Drills—Long Words

Goal: To enhance accuracy by improving concentration, thereby facilitating the typing of long words.

Features: These drills consist of words containing 12 or 13 strokes each. The sequential arrangement of the words is not in a definite stroking pattern. This will compel total concentration because it is impossible to anticipate the patterns of each word. In other words, there is a mixture of vertical strokes, alternate-hand strokes, and so on.

Line: 66 spaces

Directions: Type each line perfectly three times—not necessarily in succession, but in total. Begin a new line immediately when you make an error. Double-space between groups of three perfect lines. Because you will be typing high-stroke-intensity words, it will be advisable to spell out each word—typing letter for letter. Type all ten drills.

Drill 1

```
transcendent consequences intellectual investigation congressional
preservation relationship constituents unnecessarily necessitating
astonishment coordination requirements uncertainties accreditation
vicissitudes compromising identifiably proliferation reimbursement
```

Drill 2

```
conservative enlightening idiosyncrasy manufacturers determination
strengthened subordinates unacceptable approximately insignificant
indefinitely discriminate presidential opportunities administering
commissioner respectively overwhelming promiscuously inappropriate
```

Drill 3

```
professional confirmation distribution irresponsible mismanagement
deficiencies specifically arrangements picturesquely significantly
particularly deliberately conservative disillusioned parliamentary
anticipating accumulation quantitative authorization contradictory
```

Drill 4

```
prosecutions remuneration commercially controversies traditionally
ridiculously suppositions insinuations concentration practitioners
intimidation intervention consistently interestingly championships
neighborhood construction orchestrated international demonstration
```

Words

Individualists are those thinkers and planners, pioneers and leaders | 14
who dare to branch out into new experiences or perform experiments that | 28
reshape, alter, or change our lives. Included in this group are those who | 43
developed and expanded expertise in the field of office skills, as well as | 58
inventors, scientists, and those in other fields. | 68

My father was both a pioneer and a leader in every sense. In addition | 83
to his fame as a champion typist, he was well known for his ability to | 97
motivate others. Wherever he went, people who observed his demonstrations | 112
became so enamored that they followed him from one demonstration to another | 127
and sometimes even followed him to Washington, D.C. Consequently, he was | 142
similar to the pied piper, except his music was played on the typewriter. | 157

After watching a demonstration in Atlantic City, a young man named | 170
Frank came to Washington with the idea of becoming the next world champion | 185
typist. In fact, before seeing my father type, he thought he was already | 200
the fastest typist in the world. Like so many others, he had been living | 215
in a world of fantasy. For the first time he realized that he needed | 229
championship coaching to advance step by step from basic typing skills to | 244
an entirely new realm--championship typing. | 253

Frank was typing about eighty net words a minute on ten-minute timed | 267
writings. However, he had two serious flaws in his typing technique that | 281
prevented him from realizing his goal. First, he held his right hand too | 296
high. To a person unknowledgeable about keyboarding techniques, this would | 311
not make any difference, but to a typing expert it was a terrible mistake. | 327
Second, he could not keep his elbows down. After typing two or three | 341
minutes, he permitted both elbows to rise until his forearms were parallel | 356
to the floor. This caused him to make extra errors and lose speed. | 369
Although Frank was mentally determined to excel in typing, his failure to | 384
perfect his typing techniques kept him from becoming a champion typist. | 399

Undoubtedly, you have unused resources that have never been recognized | 413
and talents that have never been used. But if you wish to make the best | 428
possible progress in typing, you must strive to use the proper techniques-- | 443
often called championship techniques. What may appear to be an | 455
insignificant flaw in your technique can make the difference in how fast | 470
and how accurately you type. The decision is yours, but you must eliminate | 485
or overcome all obstacles that keep you from achieving the results you | 499
desire. It will not be easy, but it will certainly be worth the effort. | 514

| 1 | 2 | 3 | 4 | 5 | 6 | 7 | 8 | 9 | 10 | 11 | 12 | 13 | 14 | 15 |

Drill 5

corporation cooperation advise advice might night knight plains planes
savage salvage trough through threw thru principal principle seam seem
see sea seen scene great grate create crate site cite sight fake flake
sweater sweeter grandma grammar aid aide pair pear pare powers powders

Drill 6

stationary stationery cede seed preceding proceeding formally formerly
led lead minute minuet ingenuous ingenious addition edition loose lose
council counsel consul continual continuous dying dyeing devise device
farther further father envelop envelope capital capitol sleigh sleight

Drill 7

complement compliment inert invert invent dairy diary scar scare score
choose chose chosen fonder founder flounder troop troupe change chance
inspiring aspiring toast taste fault flaunt skin skein wrecked wracked
vain vein vine prey pray sell cell sever severe serve grander grandeur

Drill 8

hypothesis hypotheses stain strain word world thesis theses rout route
edition addition audition action auction wine wind intimate intimidate
message massage persecution prosecution banana bandana bonanza sun son
decent descent descend interior exterior inviable inviolable toll told

Drill 9

by buy bye sifting shifting preserve persevere fanatically frantically
imminent eminent nose noose decease decrease million mullion poor pour
professional processional lurch lunch fiend fried friend serial cereal
lung lunge pleading pleasing fete feet feat feast deficient sufficient

Drill 10

hall haul horse hoarse fame flame frame wane wain cause clause eye aye
obvious oblivious residential presidential quit quiet quite dire dirge
bell belle not knot write right cache catch floor flour parcel partial
lighting lightning stair stare pose poise road rode rodeo radio or oar

Drill 11

pose posse possess possession avenge revenge beat beet quarter quartet
assemble ensemble mien mine mind middle meddle muddle contact contract
poll pole cents sense fail flail colon colony sale sail soil tale tail
metal medal defied denied deer dear ail ale picking pickling prickling

Words

Time and again people came to our school for help after they had tried | 14
to gain expertise in typing and failed. This was true of Helen. For ten | 29
years after she graduated from high school, she went from school to school | 44
trying to learn to type well enough to get a position as a typist. Each | 59
time she was assured she would be successful and that it would be just a | 73
matter of time before she could type fast and accurately enough to qualify | 88
for a job. These promises all proved false, and in desperation she came to | 104
our school and asked if she were hopeless. | 112

This is not an unusual question after a history of ten years of trying | 127
and failing. However, before making any final judgment or drawing | 140
conclusions, we asked Helen to type for one minute in order that an | 154
analysis of her typing could be made. This was the real issue. | 166

After she had typed only two lines, her problems were obvious. | 179
Actually, it was comparatively easy to analyze Helen's problems and | 193
prescribe the exact course that transformed her from a frustrated failure | 208
into a contented, hard-working student. She was given certain prescribed | 223
assignments that required diligent practice. Helen far exceeded the | 236
required practicing and willingly spent at least two to three hours each | 251
day practicing at home in addition to the time spent in her class. There | 266
was a steady improvement, day by day, as she typed in class. Her whole | 280
attitude had changed from one of a defeatist to one of an optimist. | 294
Although there was an obvious struggle, she was on her way to becoming the | 309
successful typist of whom she had dreamed. | 318

About six weeks after she started, Helen was ready. She had mastered | 332
the assignments and had acquired the deftness needed to pass the | 345
examination. She arranged to take the test immediately, and the next day | 360
her smiling face verified that she had passed. No day in her life will be | 375
more momentous and seem of greater importance. Her persistence had paid | 389
off, and she had achieved the success she had sought for so many years. | 404

Helen's success depended upon, as yours will, practicing in a certain | 418
prescribed manner. There just isn't any substitute for continual | 431
practicing in the correct manner. Practicing incorrectly only compounds | 446
your problems. So attack each problem separately and repeat each problem | 460
area repeatedly until you eliminate the source of your difficulty. By | 475
consistently practicing in this manner, you will soon find your fingers | 489
flying over the keyboard quickly and accurately. | 499

| 1 | 2 | 3 | 4 | 5 | 6 | 7 | 8 | 9 | 10 | 11 | 12 | 13 | 14 | 15 |

Accuracy Study 22

Concentration Drills—Similar Words

Goal: To improve accuracy by developing absolute and complete concentration on each word to be typed.

Features: These drills contain a concentration of similar-looking or similar-sounding words, thereby compelling intense concentration.

Line: 70 spaces

Directions: Type each line perfectly three times—not necessarily in succession, but in total. Begin a new line immediately when you make an error. Double-space between groups of three perfect lines. Because concentration plays a major role in accuracy—students make more concentration errors than any other type of error—it will be necessary for you to *spell out each letter of each word.* This may cause you to reduce your typing speed initially; however, once you become accustomed to typing on a single-stroke-recognition basis, your typing speed will return to your normal rate and the number of errors you make will be reduced dramatically. Therefore, type *letter for letter.* Type each drill.

Drill 1

an and angle angel be bee bin been bend but butt butte buff bear bare
bore boar beer bier here hear hair hare flair fair fare stakes steaks
concert convert verse averse adverse disperse diverse inverse immerse
rehearse reverse clutch crutch blood flood mug smug snug defray delay

Drill 2

rub tub grub scrub club construct instruct pulse repulse engage enrage
unstrung unsung drunk dunk sunk attach attacks attack fir fur per purr
chasseur chauffeur way weigh decay delay dismay display scratch snatch
canvas canvass draft draught affect effect adopt adapt adept loan lone

Drill 3

hew new knew proceed precede succeed recede dear deer ware wear to too
wait weight wake blue blew birth berth sake shake stake except excerpt
sage stage dodge lodge fog flog back black claque plaque threw through
clack crack alack attack bake brake break fake flake fine find ail ale

Drill 4

ton tone smile simile bough bought brought sought though thought tough
closet closest formally formerly board broad forth fourth later latter
prescribe proscribe breath breathe berth birth coarse course lane lain
deserts desserts peace piece access excess their there weather whether

Supplemental Timed Writing 3

One of life's greatest pleasures is helping someone in need, — 12
especially when the recipient really appreciates it. You, too, will find — 27
that nothing will give you a greater sense of satisfaction and achievement — 42
than knowing that you have used your knowledge, skill, and ability to help — 57
others to achieve a more pleasant and rewarding way of life. — 69

The story of Mildred is not unique. It is only one success story — 83
among many others that could be written about ambitious young people who, — 98
after being reared on a farm and experiencing deprivation, went to the city — 113
to seek either fame or fortune, or, in some instances, both. However, this — 128
is a true story of a young woman named Mildred, and her problems seemed — 142
unique to her. She was one of a large family of children and had lived on — 157
a farm all her life. In fact, she had never ventured far from home. No — 172
one in her family had attended college, and she wanted to be the first. — 186

When Mildred arrived in the city, she had no money, no clothes, no — 200
friends, no place to live, and no one who could give financial assistance. — 215
She was completely on her own. However, Mildred possessed attributes that — 230
money cannot buy. She was resourceful, ambitious, and determined to — 244
achieve her goal on her own. — 250

A preliminary test at our college showed that she was qualified for a — 264
junior position in both typing and shorthand. Her typing speed and — 278
shorthand skill enabled her, a novice, to work part-time for a local — 291
newspaper as a stenographer. Mildred earned sufficient income with this — 306
part-time job to enable her to attend school and provide for other — 319
necessities. She had no luxuries--she earned barely enough to make ends — 334
meet and pay her tuition. — 339

After Mildred graduated from college, she immediately went to work for — 354
a government agency. After a period of time, she transferred to another — 368
agency, then transferred to a position in the White House. After working — 383
at the White House, she had the opportunity to work overseas. She finally — 398
returned to America and now had a well-paying government position. — 411

The story of Mildred is a fascinating, true story of a young woman — 425
who started on the lowest rung of the economic ladder and advanced until — 440
she had a prestigious position and earned an excellent salary. — 452

There is no easy road to success, but you, too, will succeed if you — 466
utilize your capabilities properly and manage your resources and time. — 480

| 1 | 2 | 3 | 4 | 5 | 6 | 7 | 8 | 9 | 10 | 11 | 12 | 13 | 14 | 15 |

Drill 3 Quotation Marks, Periods, and Commas

He said, "I am glad that you won the lottery," and I replied, "What are you going to do with all of the money that you just won?" He said, "I am going to put a lot of the money in U.S. savings bonds--for my old-age protection--and I am also going to visit New York City, Boston, Philadelphia, Chicago, Miami, and Washington, D.C. I have desired to visit those places at least once, and so it appears that I will be able to do it at long last. I shall have fun. I shall learn much. It may be worth all of the expenses involved. Why don't you come too?"

Drill 4 Dashes and Hyphens

He works on a day-to-day basis. I endeavored to send a form for out-of-town employment to a major self-help organization which is well-developed organizationally. A self-help group is an indispensable resource for the community and motivates many fair-to-middling individuals to aspire to creatively do something--no matter how small--to contribute to the welfare and well-being of our fine country. Under the circumstances it is our well-intentioned privilege to do our utmost to get a better understanding--for whatever it is worth--of what we can do in this respect. We are certain to do our very best.

Words

Life is not always a bowl of cherries. Sometimes it is very cruel,   14
and only a very strong, determined person is mentally and emotionally   28
equipped to overcome the hard knocks one experiences. Suffering and   42
adversity often strike without warning. This was true in the case of   56
William, a steady, rather studious young man.   65

William became an excellent typist after only one year of training in   79
this skill. In fact, he had achieved his personal goal in one year and   93
obtained a position as a clerk-typist. As this was the extent of his   107
ambition, he dropped out of college.   115

About a year later, William telephoned to say that he had lost the use   129
of his right hand as the result of an automobile accident. In fact, he   144
could not move his right arm at all. William had suffered a devastating   158
experience, and some fundamental changes would have to be made in his style   173
of living to enable him to adjust to the grim realities he was facing.   188

He wondered if it were possible for anyone to learn to type by using   202
only one hand. Other disabled individuals have achieved success in art,   216
music, and other professions, so the answer had to be in the affirmative.   231

William's eagerness astounded everyone. He was one of the first   244
students to register for the fall semester. From a psychological,   258
physical, and financial point of view, success was imperative. Learning   272
the keyboard, inserting the paper, and turning pages in a book were only a   287
few of the obstacles facing this young man. The major problem was to   301
develop speed and accuracy comparable to others who had two hands.   315

William requested approval to take a concentrated typing course, and   329
in addition, he requested permission to practice during a three-and-a-half-   344
hour interval between day and evening classes. Permission was granted, and   359
William practiced diligently and faithfully every single day. His   372
diligence and determination paid off, for at the end of the school year, he   387
passed a typing examination and got an excellent position.   399

At graduation, William received a gold medallion in recognition of his   414
extraordinary courage and display of perseverance. This incident from real   429
life should point out that a shattering blow need not destroy one but can   444
be a stepping-stone to other goals. William proved the proverb that says,   459
"Where there is a will, there is a way." If William could learn to type   473
with the use of only one hand, you can certainly learn to type too if you   488
will exert sufficient effort.   494

| 1 | 2 | 3 | 4 | 5 | 6 | 7 | 8 | 9 | 10 | 11 | 12 | 13 | 14 | 15 |

Accuracy Study 21

Punctuation

DO NOT LOOK AT YOUR KEYBOARD

Goal: To improve accuracy in typing punctuation marks.

Features: These drills contain a concentration of various punctuation marks. Each drill emphasizes two or more punctuation marks, and this emphasis is clearly indicated in each drill.

Line: 65 spaces

Directions: Type each line of the paragraph perfectly three times—not necessarily in succession, but in total—of each drill that has punctuation marks on which you made too many errors in the Pretest. Begin a new line immediately when you make an error. Double-space between groups of three perfect lines.

Drill 1   Commas and Periods

```
The girls saw birds, dogs, cats, sheep, cows, bulls, goats,
chickens, roosters, ducks, turkeys, rabbits, and a goose on
my brother's farm.  They, it seems to me, were surprised to
see a variety of crops growing:  corn, potatoes, beans, bib
lettuce, cucumbers, cantaloupes, watermelons, kale, onions,
celery, spinach, cabbage, collard greens, and squash.  This
was quite an educational experience for them.  It was great
fun and something they would be able to tell their friends.
```

Drill 2   Question Marks, Periods, and Exclamation Points

```
Who is it?  It is I.  What do you want?  I want to talk to
you.  What about?  Open the door and find out.  Why should
I?  It is important!  How can I know that it is important?
Well, you know me and I would not say it if it was not so!
All right, then, I will open the door.  I am glad that you
did.  Why?  You won first prize in the raffle drawing that
the state conducted last night.  First prize, as you know,
is a trip around the world traveling first class on one of
the best airplanes anywhere.  It's worth opening the door!
```

Words

A positive attitude is one of the greatest assets you can possess. 14
Guard it carefully. Progress and success, whether in the classroom, on the 29
job, or at home, are affected by it. Your attitude reveals your readiness 44
to assume the responsibilities involved in a job or in social contacts. 58

Examine your inner self critically to ensure that no negative 71
tendencies intrude. If you have a martyr complex and foster feelings of 86
inferiority or if you make excuses for poor work or for too little done, 100
you are rationalizing deficiencies. Other negative traits that drain you 115
of vitality, rob you of efficiency, and dull your brain power are 128
depression, tension, irritation, and intolerance. Your attitude toward 143
your fellow classmates or workers, toward supervision, and toward 156
responsibility is as important as your attitude about yourself. 169

Psychologists tell us that attitude is an enduring structure of 182
beliefs that causes us to behave selectively toward physical objects, 196
events, and behavior. Thus, we conclude that a positive mental concept of 211
our ability and worth is extremely important in striving toward a goal. 225
Conversely, it is impossible to progress satisfactorily in work or live a 240
meaningful life if one is filled with negative perceptions. 252

Perception of yourself is a powerful force that influences and guides 266
you. If you perceive yourself as becoming a successful typist, you will 281
see yourself as responsible for your progress. You will pinpoint what you 296
do, or fail to do, that causes your success or failure. You will reinforce 311
your attainments and correct your errors. You know that you guide your 325
destiny in typing. Since you perceive that you are competent, you will 340
invest your time, energy, and talents in full measure today so you may reap 355
the benefits of a superior typing skill tomorrow. 365

Typing is one of the most important ways of conveying information. 379
You, the typist, will be judged by the quality of the product produced, and 394
your attitude will be displayed by your work. 403

Two of the most important aspects of a positive attitude are interest 417
and desire. If you are interested, you will absorb more information from 432
your surroundings, and you will become aware of opportunities that further 447
your goal. Desire will make you more creative. These attitudes make you 462
search for new opportunities and new approaches to implement ideas. A 476
person with a positive attitude reflects a sense of accomplishment and 490
radiates an infectious enthusiasm in every endeavor. 501

| 1 | 2 | 3 | 4 | 5 | 6 | 7 | 8 | 9 | 10 | 11 | 12 | 13 | 14 | 15 |

Accuracy Study 20

Right-Hand Words

Goal: To enhance accuracy in typing by developing much better control of all the fingers of the right hand.

Features: These drills employ a systematic approach for perfecting reaches involving the fingers of the right hand. There is a concentration of difficult words in each line, so as you develop fluency in typing them, you will notice a corresponding improvement in your accuracy and finger dexterity.

Line: 75 spaces

Directions: Type each line perfectly three times—not necessarily in succession, but in total. Begin a new line immediately when you make an error. Double-space between groups of three perfect lines. Begin typing very slowly, and gradually increase your typing rate until you are typing at your fastest accurate rate. Type all three drills.

Drill 1   H, I, J, and K

```
hippopotamus hokum haphazard humor hilum hilly homonym humanize homonyms
initiate inimitable injustice ionic iniquity injurious idiosyncrasy inky
jeopardize jerkily junk jumpy jujitsu junction jolly jalousie jalopy jut
kimono knowledge kilometer knuckles kick kind khaki kayak kamikaze kills
```

Drill 2   L, M, N, and O

```
lackadaisically luminescent limited lumpy lolly lazily loyalty loop loin
magnanimity monopoly minimum maximum minikin monotonous murmurous murmur
numinous nihility numbs nylon nozzle napalm number nominee nihilism nook
optimum oilily olympians ominous olympic opinions opposition opportunity
```

Drill 3   P, U, and Y

```
poliomyelitis pump pumpkin puny portrait population points physical puppy
ultimatum usual unusual union upon uphold unruly unscrupulous unambiguous
yolk yipped yellowy youth yourselves yokel yacht yardage young yesteryear
```

Training in keyboarding is a great character developer. It requires a 14
mixture of pliability, perseverance, discipline, and honesty to achieve 29
this important motor skill. You must develop all these characteristics if 44
you wish to master and excel in typing. It also takes a great deal of 58
human intelligence and human will to apply the basic mechanics. Typing is 73
not an easy skill, and to achieve success, you must set realistic goals. 88
You may, after an honest self-analysis, be compelled to admit that your 102
goals need to be redefined. 108

You must educate yourself both in class and out of class. Typing 121
skill is not free. It is not something you receive or have presented to 136
you as a gift. The only way in which you can obtain it is to want it 150
enough to pay for it with your own efforts. You must earn this skill, just 165
as you must earn everything else that is really valuable to you. 178

You, more than anyone else, determine how fast you will acquire typing 192
proficiency. No matter how much and how well you are taught, no matter 207
what opportunities you have for learning, you will gain almost nothing 221
unless you take an active interest in remedying your deficiencies. These 236
timed writings will reveal your strong points and your weak points and will 251
emphasize what you need to practice to gain proficiency. 262

A real desire to learn serves as a "self-starter." It will give you a 277
driving motive toward a definite goal. It will keep your mind alert, and 292
practicing will become more interesting, even exciting. Without waiting to 307
be taught, you should make every effort to attain mastery of this important 322
skill. If you gain skill in managing yourself and your time and in 336
disciplining your mind, you will make rapid progress. 346

Unfortunately, some students lack skill in typing because they have 360
not trained themselves to study efficiently. You cannot plod rather 374
blindly through crucial typing assignments day after day and hope to make 389
spectacular progress. If you muddle along--wasting your time and energy-- 404
you will become discouraged. It is necessary that you study proper skill- 419
development strategies. 424

Frustrations are a part of becoming an expert typist. To attain 437
typing proficiency, your fingers must respond automatically to the impulse 452
of your brain. If you dedicate yourself to a high standard of perfection 467
in your practicing, you will soon be transformed into a superior typist. 481

| 1 | 2 | 3 | 4 | 5 | 6 | 7 | 8 | 9 | 10 | 11 | 12 | 13 | 14 | 15 |

Accuracy Study 19

Left-Hand Words

DO NOT LOOK AT YOUR FINGERS

Goal: To enhance accuracy in typing by developing much better control of all the fingers of the left hand.

Features: These drills employ a systematic approach for mastering reaches involving the fingers of the left hand. Many of the words contained in these drills are difficult to type. As you develop fluency in typing them, you will notice a marked improvement in your finger dexterity and accuracy.

Line: 75 spaces

Directions: Type each line perfectly three times—not necessarily in succession, but in total. Begin a new line immediately when you make an error. Double-space between groups of three perfect lines. Begin each line slowly, gradually increasing your typing rate on each subsequent line until you have reached your fastest accurate typing rate. Type all four drills.

Drill 1 A, B, C, and D

abstracter achievable acquisitive analyzable attributable azaleas attest
battered badgered baggages beatable bibliography believably benedictions
combining cabaret cabbages ceded cubic criminologists created categorize
decedent desegregate deeded dazzled dissatisfied dependence debate dazed

Drill 2 E, F, G, and Q

exacerbate extravaganza eczema erasable exceeded exactly equate excerpts
fabric fragrance freeze freezer federate fragmentation fateful frustrate
galaxy gaze gigantic garage garbage grazes greatest gregarious gravitate
quarrels quarry quantity quackery quench quandary quagmire quadruplicate

Drill 3 R, S, T, and V

recede reverberate reveille regrettable rebellion rebate reaction regret
staggered squatters segregated sextet swerved sewage seesaw sequence sew
tumultuous terrestrial twist tweezer traverse tranquility tattoo tatters
visualize vex vast vertex vertigo vertebra vegetables vegetate venerable

Drill 4 W, X, and Z

waterer watering watcher wasps warrantable weave waltz whiz warble wafter
axe axiomatic extreme exceed exalt exception extra expeditious exorbitant
zinnia zinc zonally zealous zeroes zany zealot zigzag zigzagging zoophyte

Words

The proper mental attitude is essential if one wishes to learn to type. In fact, without the proper attitude, learning this skill will be difficult and will result in an unnecessarily frustrating experience.

When observing a champion typist key rapidly and apparently effortlessly, one might well conclude that typing is a comparatively easy skill to acquire. Appearances are tremendously deceptive in this respect. Perhaps you can remember quite vividly the difficulty you had initially in learning the keyboard. One needs only to study the conditions under which the old masters perfected typing techniques to realize that it is impossible to achieve success in typing without using the proper techniques and without dedicated hard work. Histories of successful people--typists and others--illustrate all too clearly the lessons of patience and the efforts of years of practice and discipline.

However, typing does not have to be too difficult if you will learn the right way to practice. In fact, the championship way you are now studying is indeed the best way and the simplest way to learn to type. You must realize that typing is a skill with many facets, and in order to acquire this skill, you must use a wide variety of practice procedures. The proper typing techniques were developed by the old masters of typing over a period of many years. These old masters made a very comprehensive study of the various typing motions and developed the most expeditious way of making every stroke and motion in typing. You are learning their methods, and if you will follow instructions precisely, do exactly what you are told, and type these drills faithfully and conscientiously, your success as an expert typist is assured.

Another ingredient that is essential is absolute self-confidence. You must assume that you are going to succeed in order to learn to type. One of the surest ways to succeed in typing lies in thoroughness. This means that you must decide that you are going to master typing, that you will practice exactly as you are instructed, and that you will practice diligently no matter how difficult it seems or how much time is required. In typing, a regard for the small things is necessary. If you can overcome small worries, you will soon override the greater obstacles you encounter.

It is true that some people become successful typists in less time than others, but in every instance, putting in much hard work and developing the correct typing techniques guarantee success.

| 13 |
| 28 |
| 42 |
| 54 |
| 69 |
| 84 |
| 99 |
| 114 |
| 127 |
| 143 |
| 157 |
| 172 |
| 181 |
| 194 |
| 208 |
| 224 |
| 238 |
| 252 |
| 267 |
| 282 |
| 297 |
| 310 |
| 326 |
| 339 |
| 347 |
| 362 |
| 377 |
| 391 |
| 406 |
| 419 |
| 434 |
| 449 |
| 464 |
| 478 |
| 491 |
| 503 |

| 1 | 2 | 3 | 4 | 5 | 6 | 7 | 8 | 9 | 10 | 11 | 12 | 13 | 14 | 15 |

Accuracy Study 18

Right Hand, Fourth Finger

Goal: To improve accuracy in typing by developing better control of the fourth finger of the right hand.

Features: This drill employs a systematic approach for mastering reaches involving the fourth finger. The words selected for this drill contain letters that are struck by the fourth finger as well as specific reaches on which many students make errors.

Line: 60 spaces

Directions: Type each line perfectly three times—not necessarily in succession, but in total. Begin a new line immediately when you make an error. Double-space between groups of three perfect lines. Begin typing each line slowly, and gradually increase your typing speed.

Drill 1   P Stroke

```
package pacific painstaking papaya pajamas pageants papillon
phase pharmacy pheasant phonics pharmacist phenomenal pauses
piano pianist piazza pin pamper pica picador picadors pickle
points poinsettia poisons poisonous pole polemics population
```

Words

Developing speed in typing is one of the most difficult things to — 13
accomplish. Two of the major factors in developing speed are perfecting — 28
your keystroking techniques and keying at a smooth rate. The third most — 43
important way to develop speed is by keying the diagnostic sentences, which — 58
have been specially structured to determine weaknesses in stroke patterns. — 73
I collected statistical data over a three-year period to ascertain speed — 88
norms at varying speeds. If you find that you are deficient in speed on — 102
any of the stroke combinations, you merely have to practice those stroke — 117
combinations until you can key them fluently. It would be a good idea to — 132
key each sentence that causes you speed deficiencies ten times and then — 146
practice the necessary drills as indicated. — 155

You will find that as you become more fluent in keying those stroke — 169
combinations, your speed will increase. Of course, just keying the drills — 184
nonchalantly will be of no value at all. It is only conscientious — 197
practicing that will be meaningful. You must have the right mind-set in — 212
order to become a good typist. The faster you key, the harder you will — 226
have to labor in order to make good progress. If you are a beginning — 240
typing student, you may only have to key a line three times in order to — 254
make good progress. If you are an intermediate typing student, you will — 269
have to practice a particular sentence five times in order to make — 282
satisfactory progress. However, if you are an advanced typing student, you — 298
may have to key a sentence ten times to make progress. — 309

As you improve your skills, and reach higher and higher speed levels, — 323
you may find that words which were not problems for you to key at lower — 337
speed rates are becoming problems as your speed increases. It takes a — 351
great deal of determination to become a proficient typist and, as I said — 366
before, a lot of good character in order to excel in this discipline. — 380

Fortunately for you, you are following the trail of world champion — 394
typists, and I am carefully guiding you around the many pitfalls that you — 408
would ordinarily face. However, you have a major role to play; you must — 423
exhibit zest and enthusiasm every day possible. To excel in this — 436
discipline, practice your drills, take your timed writings, and fully — 450
cooperate with your teacher. Make up your mind--right now if you have not — 465
already done so--to give the mastery of this skill your very best effort. — 480
Then you will really succeed. — 486

| 1 | 2 | 3 | 4 | 5 | 6 | 7 | 8 | 9 | 10 | 11 | 12 | 13 | 14 | 15 |

Accuracy Study 17

Left Hand, Fourth Finger

Goal: To improve accuracy in typing by developing better control of the fourth finger of the left hand.

Features: These drills employ a systematic approach for perfecting reaches involving the fourth finger. The words contained in these drills not only include a number of letters involving the fourth finger but, in addition, emphasize specific reaches on which many students make errors.

Line: 60 spaces

Directions: Type each line perfectly three times—not necessarily in succession, but in total. Begin a new line immediately when you make an error. Double-space between groups of three perfect lines. Start typing each line slowly, and gradually increase your typing tempo.

Drill 1   Q Stroke

```
quadrennial quadrennium quadrilateral quadrille quench quest
quadrumvirate quadruped quadruple quadruplets quadruplicates
qualifier qualm quality quantal quantifiable quantifications
quantity quarter quarantine quarantinable quarrel queasiness
```

Drill 2   A Stroke

```
a at attack attribute attributable attire attach attachments
act acts actions accompany acquires acquisition acquisitions
as ash ashamed ashore ascend ascension ascribe astonishments
awake awaken aware awareness awesome azaleas azimuth azurite
```

Drill 3   Z Stroke

```
zip zipped zipping zippers zippy zircons zirconate zirconium
zirconic zithers zizith zodiac zombi zonal zonate zone zones
zoo zoomorphic zoogenic zoogeography zoological zoology zoom
zoophyte zonally zounds zygote zeppelins zymotic zygomorphic
```

Words

One of the most important techniques a typist possesses is the ability | 14
to key at a smooth, rhythmic pace. If you are keying in a herky-jerky | 29
manner, you are keying incorrectly and you will have a very difficult time | 44
in meeting the competencies. You must learn to key smoothly. The best way | 59
to key smoothly is to key along with me on the rhythm tapes I have made. | 73

I had the advantage of keying with a world champion typist when I was | 88
learning to key. And that wonderful learning experience I enjoyed, I have | 103
duplicated on my tapes. Your goal is to match me stroke for stroke, with | 117
perfect rhythm and with perfect accuracy. You will notice that as you | 132
become proficient in keying with the tapes, you will become more proficient | 147
in accuracy and speed on the timings. Therefore, you must strive for | 161
absolute perfection or come as close to perfection as possible. | 174

If you find a word, a phrase, or a sentence that causes you problems | 188
in accuracy or rhythm, practice that problem area many times. You may have | 203
to practice the same problem several days before you master it. But you | 217
must persist, as learning a good keyboarding skill is not easy. It will be | 233
well worth all the effort you put into it. It is good practice that | 246
produces good results. Therefore, always do your best. It will certainly | 261
pay off for you later in life. | 268

Another important aspect of keyboarding is keying at a smooth, | 280
rhythmic pace. It is the continuity of stroking that enables one to key at | 296
a very fast and accurate rate. I find nothing in keyboarding as irritating | 311
and disgusting as hearing a person keying in a herky-jerky manner. I know | 326
that person is keying very inaccurately as well as with insufficient speed. | 341
I was very fortunate to have had a world champion sit beside me and key | 356
with me at a predetermined pace. This enabled me to progress at a very | 370
rapid rate. | 372

Due to the advancement in technology, I have been able to duplicate | 386
the wonderful learning experience I shared with my father by making several | 401
sets of rhythm keyboarding tapes. These tapes begin at the rate of twenty | 416
words a minute and graduate to sixty-five words a minute. | 428

An excellent way to develop your speed and accuracy is to use the | 441
audio cassette tapes regularly. The utilization of these tapes will | 455
produce simply amazing results. I used these tapes with my students, and, | 470
as a consequence, most of them could key five minutes without making more | 485
than one misstroke. | 489

| 1 | 2 | 3 | 4 | 5 | 6 | 7 | 8 | 9 | 10 | 11 | 12 | 13 | 14 | 15 |

Accuracy Study 16

Right Hand, Third Finger

KEEP EYES ON COPY

Goal: To enhance accuracy in typing by developing better control of the third finger of the right hand.

Features: These drills employ a systematic approach for mastering reaches involving the third finger. The words that have been selected not only contain a number of letters involving the third finger but, equally important, stress particular reaches on which many students make errors.

Line: 60 spaces

Directions: Type each line perfectly three times—not necessarily in succession, but in total. Begin a new line immediately when you make an error. Double-space between groups of three perfect lines. Begin typing each line slowly, and gradually increase your typing speed.

Drill 1   O Stroke

```
oak obedience object oblivion occurrence occupy odors odious
onus onyx ooze oozy opal open opened opening operational out
operate operable ophite opiate opinion opinionated opportune
oppress oppression oppressive optimal optimism optimum optic
```

Drill 2   L Stroke

```
label labor lap laborious labyrinth lapidary laconic lacquer
lazy lazily lament laxation lexicon layette lead leaf ledger
limp library lying liege lien like lilies limited limitation
loxodrome lucid lucidity ludicrous lug luggage lullaby lulls
```

Words

Most people find that in typing they make too many misstrokes because 14
they find that their minds wander while they are keying. This is a common 29
phenomenon. It is so easy to see someone's name and immediately begin to 44
think about the person. That is one of the worst things you can do, 58
because while your concentration is broken, you will key many "toads." 72

The word toad is an acronym for concentration misstrokes. It covers 86
these common misstrokes: transpositions, omissions, additions, and 100
doubling of the wrong letter. Anytime one of these errors occurs, it is a 115
concentration misstroke. After being in the classroom for more than thirty 130
years, I have found that the best way to eliminate toads is by keying on a 145
letter-recognition basis--that is, keying letter for letter. Spell out 159
each word as you key it, and key with good rhythm. If you find a word, a 174
phrase, or a sentence that causes you to hesitate or even make a misstroke, 189
key that incorrect word correctly twenty-five times. Amazingly, you will 204
find that response to making misstrokes very effective in correcting that 219
problem and upgrading your overall typing skills. 229

Once you key on a letter-for-letter basis, you will find that your 242
concentration will be greatly enhanced. You will also find that it is 257
relatively easy to key rhythmically, and that is a vitally important 270
technique for you to perfect. The syllabic intensity is irrelevant when 285
you key on a letter basis. Your misstrokes will also be greatly reduced 300
and your speed in typing will be greatly increased as soon as you get 314
accustomed to keying on a letter-for-letter basis. 324

Those students who follow my advice usually become excellent typists. 338
Since you are in this class, you may just as well do everything the correct 353
way so you can make excellent progress, because to do everything another 368
way probably will cause you to have a horrendous experience. A person who 383
follows expert advice is the person who usually excels in whatever 396
undertaking he or she pursues. Generally, I have observed that a person 411
who excels in one endeavor will usually excel in another. I am certain 425
that you, too, wish to excel, and that is why you are learning to type. 440
You realize that the computer will play--if it has not already done so--a 455
major role in your life. Most likely, that is exactly why you are in this 470
class right now. So why not do your best? 478

| 1 | 2 | 3 | 4 | 5 | 6 | 7 | 8 | 9 | 10 | 11 | 12 | 13 | 14 | 15 |

Accuracy Study 15

Left Hand, Third Finger

Goal: To enhance accuracy in typing by developing better control of the third finger of the left hand.

Features: These drills employ a systematic approach for perfecting reaches involving the third finger. The words selected for these drills contain letters that are struck by the third finger and reinforce basic reaches on which many students make errors.

Line: 60 spaces

Directions: Type each line perfectly three times—not necessarily in succession, but in total. Begin a new line immediately when you make an error. Double-space between groups of three perfect lines. Start typing each line slowly, and gradually increase your typing tempo.

Drill 1   W Stroke

wade wader wafer waft wafter wag wagging wagon wage waif was

waist waive walk ward war ware wasp warrantable washer watch

web weevil weft weeping welfare wench west wet western weeps

wrest wrench wrestle wriggle wrinkle wrist writ writing whip

Drill 2   S Stroke

saber sabbatical sacrifice sag sagacity safety sanctimonious

scalp scallop scarce scarf scavenger scintillate scissor sew

squabble squad squalor square squash squat squatters squawks

steeve steer stencil sterilize stitches stiltedly stipulates

Drill 3   X Stroke

extreme exceed exaction exceeding exceedingly exalt excepted

exception exceptional excise external externally externalize

excerpt exonerate exorbitant exorcism exoteric explicit exit

extra extreme extrication expedite expeditious expel expiate

Words

Another serious problem many students experience is the anxiety of 14
having to take a test. Nervousness is one of the most serious problems to 29
overcome. I had a student who had the worst case of nervousness I have 43
ever seen. Just the mention of a test would cause him to have palpitations 58
of the heart; wet, sweaty hands; and jitters. Rickey could not sit still 73
whenever he had to take a test. 79

During ordinary practicing, Rickey had good techniques, good rhythm, 93
and apparently all the attributes of a good typist. However, once he knew 108
he had to take a five-minute timing, Rickey would seemingly come apart. 123

When I was fourteen, I demonstrated my typing skill at my junior high. 137
My mother and about five hundred students were there. My heart rate 151
accelerated rapidly, my palms became wet, and my breathing became irregular 166
when the time arrived for the demonstration. Afterward, I wondered how my 181
father could stand it. Later that school year, I was in my first typing 196
contest, and once again, I had the same experience. However, the next 210
year, I did not. I had become immune to pressure. 220

This program is so structured that you are taking timings every single 235
day. Consequently, it is just a matter of time until you get adjusted to 250
taking timings. Sooner or later, you will be accustomed to taking timed 264
writings, and then you will be able to take a timed writing anytime or 278
anywhere. And once that occurs, all the physical manifestations that 292
Rickey experienced will pass away. Then you will be able to key without 307
any problems of anxiety again. That is what happened to Rickey as well as 322
to hundreds of other students. 328

Around the fourth week of the program, Rickey had taken so many timed 342
writings that he had become used to taking them, so he could relax and also 358
key exceedingly well. You just have to take repeated timings until you are 373
no longer nervous. If you are like Rickey, just make up your mind that you 388
will take test after test until you no longer have a problem in taking 402
them. Once you master taking tests in typing, it will help you in taking 417
tests in other fields of endeavor. However, every time you practice or 431
take a timing, you must do your very best because only good practice 445
produces good results. You cannot fail if you come to class every day and 460
always do your best. 464

| 1 | 2 | 3 | 4 | 5 | 6 | 7 | 8 | 9 | 10 | 11 | 12 | 13 | 14 | 15 |

Accuracy Study 14

Right Hand, Second Finger

Goal: To improve accuracy in typing by developing better control of the second finger of the right hand.

Features: These drills employ a systematic approach for mastering reaches involving the second finger. The words contained in these drills not only include a number of letters involving the second finger but also emphasize specific reaches on which many students make errors.

Line: 60 spaces

Directions: Type each line perfectly three times—not necessarily in succession, but in total. Begin a new line immediately when you make an error. Double-space between groups of three perfect lines. Begin each line slowly, and gradually increase your typing rate.

Drill 1   I Stroke

```
ilex ill ilium illegal illegitimate illness illustrative ilk
image imagery imaginable imbalance imitates iniquities imbue
ink inmate innate inning innocence innuendo inquisition inky
irresistibility irrigate irritable irritant itemization itch
```

Drill 2   K Stroke

```
kaddish kaiser kayak kale kaleidoscope kamikaze kangaroo key
keel keen keep keeper keeping kennel kernel kerosene kettles
king kingdom kingly kink kinsfolk kip kismet kiss kisses kit
kitchen kite kitten kleptomaniac knack knap knave knee known
```

Drill 3   E and I Strokes

```
counterfeit retrieve protein hierarchy caffeine anxiety heir
spontaneity lien leisure believe kaleidoscopic alien freight
achieve deceit relieve foreign reprieve forfeited brief rein
heinous science surveillance friend reimburse relief receive
```

Words

In order to be successful in any endeavor, you must have a positive | 14
attitude. It is so much easier to accomplish anything when you believe you | 29
can do it. With each timed writing, you will be encouraged to upgrade your | 44
skills, and in order to accomplish that feat, you must believe in your | 58
abilities. You will excel if you practice your drills faithfully and with | 73
zest. But in addition to practicing conscientiously, you must have supreme | 89
confidence in yourself. I have found it a good idea--and I believe you | 103
will also find it a good idea--to tell myself before starting a timing: I | 118
can do it! You must tell yourself this over and over again. You will be | 133
surprised to see that you will achieve your goal more often than not. | 147

You will find, as I did, that you will only get out of typing what you | 161
put into it, and you can never predict how the energy and efforts put into | 176
one area will impact other areas as well. When I began typing at the age | 191
of twelve, I had no idea that I would become one of the fastest typists of | 206
all time, a teacher, and author of the all-time best-selling skill | 219
enhancement book on typing. If you will put your best effort into this | 234
project, you will certainly get the best out of it. The same is true in | 248
whatever else you begin. Had I not had the right mind-set and practiced | 263
faithfully and enthusiastically, I would not have achieved all that I have. | 278

So a positive mind-set impacts positively on your attitude and your | 292
behavior. If you wish to succeed, you must believe you can. I never | 306
allowed my students to tell me that they could not do it. That is | 319
inexcusable. My students may say that something is difficult to achieve, | 334
but with hard work and a positive attitude, they will succeed. You will be | 349
just as successful as my students were if you are determined to make an | 364
effort to be positive and to apply yourself daily. | 374

Therefore, mastering this discipline is a character developer. The | 388
attributes that contribute to your success in this enterprise will stand | 402
you in good stead in other activities. I know it to be true in my case, | 417
and I imagine it will be true for you too. I hope you have assumed a | 431
positive attitude and that you have the determination, patience, and | 445
dedication to do your best keying every day you come into this class. If | 460
so, I know you will master this competency as well as the rest of the | 474
competencies facing you. | 478

| 1 | 2 | 3 | 4 | 5 | 6 | 7 | 8 | 9 | 10 | 11 | 12 | 13 | 14 | 15 |

Accuracy Study 13

Left Hand, Second Finger

Goal: To increase accuracy in typing by developing better control of the second finger of the left hand.

Features: These drills employ a systematic approach for perfecting reaches involving the second finger. Great care has been taken in selecting words that not only contain a number of letters that are struck by the second finger but also reinforce specific reaches on which many students make errors.

Line: 60 spaces

Directions: Type each line perfectly three times—not necessarily in succession, but in total. Begin a new line immediately when you make an error. Double-space between groups of three perfect lines. Start each line slowly, and gradually increase your typing tempo.

Drill 1   E Stroke

```
eager ear eagle earl easy early easement earth earn ease eat
edema edge edginess edible edict edification education edify
era erase erasable errors eradicable erupt erratic eradicate
exact exaction exceed exalt extreme except exception extinct
```

Drill 2   D Stroke

```
dab dabble dad daffodil daffy dainty daiquiri daily dangling
debonair debrief debris debutante debt debenture debate deal
drawn drawer dread dreary dream dredge dribble dress dresser
divide dividend divisive dock docket doctrine divulge doctor
```

Drill 3   C Stroke

```
credit creatures creative creation credible credence cranial
cube cubes cubic cubicles cuckoo cucumber cart carts carried
chain chair chaise chafe chalk chalet charter champion catch
cast castle casket category cashew cater catalog coax coaxed
```

Words

Perseverance--the ability to persist despite obstacles, frustration, | 14
discouragement, and opposition--is a quality every good typist possesses. | 29
Do not become discouraged when your fingers won't do what you want them to | 44
do. Typing is a skill that presents countless opportunities for errors. A | 59
word may be omitted, letters transposed, spaces skipped, or capitals | 73
missed. However, if you will remember to economize your arm and body | 87
motions, to use the tip of each finger to strike keys, and to keep your | 101
hands relaxed and your wrists steady and low, you will be headed toward | 116
high-speed typing. | 120

Words are used to portray ideas and provide the reader with mental | 133
pictures. You will certainly have a feeling of accomplishment when you | 148
achieve the ability to think of words and have your fingers react | 161
automatically and precisely by typing them perfectly and quickly. Just | 175
imagine for a moment that your thoughts are being immediately transmitted | 190
onto your paper as your fingers fly through the air, landing squarely and | 205
quickly on the correct keys. This marvelous experience and exhilarating | 219
feeling are worth the many hours spent in acquiring this magnificent skill. | 235

To become an accurate, speedy typist is not as difficult as you might | 249
imagine. Yet you must persist in applying the correct typing techniques if | 264
you do not want to be trapped by poor posture, improper hand position, and | 279
incorrect fingering. Much of the strain of typing comes from improper | 293
finger motion and hesitation in locating the proper keys. Of equal | 307
importance is being able to identify the particular problem you have in | 321
speed or accuracy development. The best way to discover these typing areas | 336
of weakness is by using the sophisticated diagnostic charts that are a part | 352
of this championship keyboarding program. If you practice the drills | 366
developed to correct the weaknesses that were revealed from your Timed | 380
Writing and Diagnostic Test, you will make rapid progress because you are | 395
concentrating your efforts on only those areas in which you are | 407
experiencing difficulty. | 412

Another way to regain your typing composure on a topsy-turvy day is to | 427
turn to the one-minute paragraphs and practice the first paragraph until | 441
you can type it perfectly in one minute. Then type another paragraph until | 457
you have perfected it in one minute, then another and another, until you | 471
have acquired mastery of the keyboard again. You will be amazed at how | 486
this method will enhance your typing ability. | 495

| 1 | 2 | 3 | 4 | 5 | 6 | 7 | 8 | 9 | 10 | 11 | 12 | 13 | 14 | 15 |

Drill 5   H Stroke

habit hack haggle harper hamper handle handicap haunt hanger
hinge hint hip hippopotamus history historicize hither hitch
hoard hoarse hoary hoatzin hoax hokum hobble hoise hoist hit
hurt hunt hunger hump hurdle humpy hunter hurl humiliate hip

Drill 6   N Stroke

names naive named napalm narcissism narratives nation narrow
never nebulous neutrons nemesis necessary neurotic nefarious
nice nicety niche nigh night nihilism nihility nip nipper no
noble nocturn nocturnal nominal nominee nod nook noon noodle

Everyone's life is measured by time--minutes, hours, and years. A 14
giant clock in one of our largest cities has one hand that extends almost 28
six yards and weighs a ton, and although this hand moves twenty yards each 43
hour, its movement is barely visible. Symbolically, the movement of the 58
hands on a clock should remind us that wasted minutes and hours are lost 73
forever; they can never be retrieved. 80

Yesterday is history; tomorrow may never come. Today--actually, only 94
this moment--belongs to you. You are the product today of how wisely you 109
used the minutes, hours, and days that are past. Your success tomorrow 124
will be the direct result of how you utilize your time today. Your whole 138
future depends upon overcoming problems and surmounting barriers that may 153
hinder your progress. By using every hour effectively, you steadily move 168
toward a satisfactory work situation and increase your efficiency. 181

If you consciously direct your efforts toward achieving a desired end, 196
you are sure to succeed. Without a goal, there can be no struggle; without 211
struggle, there can be no victory. You must devise a specific plan or goal 226
and work toward it. Until this plan is formulated, you have nothing to 241
reach for and no way of knowing when you have achieved your goal. 254

Everyone likes action, yet some people become lazy and waste time the 268
moment they arrive at work. This deficiency cannot be overcome unless you 283
discipline yourself aggressively. You stand in the midst of fundamental 298
choices. Reason does not work automatically nor is thinking a mechanical 312
process. Of your own volition, you must set your standards and your code 327
of values and work toward living up to them. 336

If you allow yourself to settle for less than your full ability, decay 351
sets in. Your mind is the driver of your fingers, and you must drive as 365
far as your mind will take you, with excellence as your goal. Individuals 380
who merely coast are at the mercy of unknown elements. Through sacrifice 395
of leisure time and hard work, you will succeed in excelling in typing, and 410
pride will be part of your reward. 417

Every act of your life has to be willed. Thus you can rise as far in 431
typing skills as you are willing, but you must pay for this in time and 446
energy. The choice is yours to make. The choice should be the dedication 461
of yourself to your highest potential. As you progress, you will feel the 476
personal satisfaction that everyone feels after doing a job well. 489

| 1 | 2 | 3 | 4 | 5 | 6 | 7 | 8 | 9 | 10 | 11 | 12 | 13 | 14 | 15 |

Accuracy Study 12

Right Hand, First Finger

STRIKE SPACE BAR WITH RIGHT THUMB

Goal: To improve accuracy in typing by developing better control of the forefinger of the right hand.

Features: These drills employ a systematic approach for mastering reaches involving the index finger. The words that have been selected not only contain a number of letters involving the forefinger but also reinforce specific reaches on which many students make errors.

Line: 60 spaces

Directions: Type each line perfectly three times—not necessarily in succession, but in total. Begin a new line immediately when you make an error. Double-space between groups of three perfect lines. Begin each line slowly, and gradually increase your typing rate.

Drill 1   U Stroke

unaffected unaccustomed unadulterated unaware unbeaten ultra
unruly unruliness unquiet unquestioning unprecedented upsets
upon uphold upholster upholstery upkeep upper upright unions
unscientific unsheathe unsophisticated unusual unsought used

Drill 2   J Stroke

jab jack jacket jade jaded jaguar jalousie jalopy jazzy jams
jealous jealousy jeer jell jelly jeopardy jeopardize jerkily
jinx jitter jobber jockey jocose jocular jogs joiner joiners
journey jubilee judges judgment judicial juggle juggler jugs

Drill 3   M Stroke

machine machinery mad madam magazine magnanimous magnanimity
milium mimic milo mimicry mincing minimal minimization minus
mines minuet minute mock mobilize modify mogul moll mortgage
monolithic monotony monotonous monument monumental momentary

Drill 4   Y Stroke

yes yean years yearling yearn yeast yells yellow yelp yeasty
yerk yesterday yesteryear yet yew yelper yearly yearning yap
yamen yammer yarrow yare yauld yaw yawn yawning yellowy yews
yellowish yachting yardarms yauld yaupon yolked yolky yokels

Words

Quality, not quantity, should be the first objective in any type of   14
work. The aspect of productivity that is easy to forget is that quantity   29
without quality is valueless. Progress and success are affected to a great   44
extent by how one performs small duties. Often it is the little details   58
that form the bone and sinew of great successes. If you can be relied upon   74
to carry out small assignments carefully and accurately, you will generally   89
be relied upon to perform the greater ones. Nothing shows your character   104
as clearly as the way you do small things. If these are done in a slipshod   119
manner, no one will trust you to do the complicated, troublesome tasks.   133
The quality of your work will mark you for success or failure.   146

Sometimes one is tempted to rush through a task in a desire to save   160
time. This is a mistake. You must stay in control of every situation.   174
Rushing not only wastes time and energy but inflicts the needless burden of   190
typing many pages again and again that could have been typed perfectly the   205
first time. If you follow this lazy procedure, you are cheating yourself.   220

We all live in the midst of distractions. During almost every waking   234
moment, we are besieged by bids for our attention. Certain thoughts,   248
memories, feelings, and worries are always ready to intrude. We cannot   262
avoid them, but we can make a determined effort to shut out unrelated   276
messages that tend to distract our attention from work. To accomplish   290
this, we must concentrate on producing a quality product each time we   304
perform an assignment, whether it is a routine task or one that requires   319
total concentration.   323

It is unnecessary to allow poor-quality work to handicap one   336
throughout life. Everyone has personal assets and talents that have never   351
been realized. Talent is an innate ability, but skills are learned.   365
Typing is considered a production skill, and you alone set your level of   379
accomplishment. Never be content with partially learning typing   392
techniques, for you quickly forget what has been barely learned. The chief   407
value of your typing knowledge and skill is the practical use that you make   423
of them. Furthermore, your typing skill is closely related to other   436
aspects of your life by helping you to do your work more efficiently and to   452
live a happier and more comfortable life.   460

Your ability to type rapidly and accurately gives you a personal   473
advantage that can contribute to your position, your self-confidence, and,   488
of course, your career. Quality is your key to success.   499

| 1 | 2 | 3 | 4 | 5 | 6 | 7 | 8 | 9 | 10 | 11 | 12 | 13 | 14 | 15 |

Drill 5 G Stroke

gain gainful galaxy gaze gauge galley gang gangsters garnish
generation generic genesis genteel geography geomagnetic gem
glacial glad gladiator glare glaze glebe globe glorious glow
gaffer goggle gong gorgeous graft grass grade grab greed gas

Drill 6 B Stroke

bit bitter big bigger bike bikini bile bilingual bilk bilker
boy born borrow borough burrow boss book books blossom bloom
buffet buffer bug bugaboo bugle budget budgetary bag baggage
beatable beauty beautiful best bestiary bestow bezel bezique

Individuals perceive their work situations in numerous ways. Some 14
perceive it as drudgery. Others perceive it as a source of power over 28
others. Yet for some, work is perceived as an outlet for creativity. In 43
each case, as the perceived need is met, higher-level needs emerge and 57
influence the behavior of the individual. 65

Your work will be either satisfying or frustrating, depending upon 79
your ability to function capably with other people and in a variety of 93
situations. A certain amount of frustration, anxiety, self-doubt, or 107
indifference may be expected, but these need not give you a feeling of 121
inadequacy. In fact, as you recognize these symptoms, you should feel 135
challenged to fulfill the requirements of each assignment. 147

Do not expect everything in a work situation to be perfect. Most 161
people are responsible and dependable, and they put in a fair amount of 175
effort for their wages. Of course, there are exceptions; and the 188
troublemakers and chronic complainers are always more conspicuous than 202
hardworking, honest individuals. 209

In the competitive climate in which we live, more than anything else 223
you will need to use your typing talent to the utmost, act independently 238
whenever possible, and prove your capability in this skill. Analyze and 252
evaluate your potential capabilities and typing skill. Apply all your 266
resources to improving the development and use of this talent. Good 280
planning, organization, and a respect for deadlines will win you the 294
gratitude of your supervisor and superiors. 303

You should perceive the goals of the organization as being relevant to 317
your personal objectives. You not only serve your organization, but also 332
represent your organization and your supervisor. This fact imposes serious 347
responsibilities upon you as a person and as a typist. Everything you type 362
should be as nearly perfect as possible. Occasionally, a part of your work 378
may seem to be unimportant. This work may not be important to you, but to 393
a keen observer, it may have unusual significance. Always remember that 407
your typing provides someone with a permanent record of the important 421
decisions and functions of your organization. 430

A renowned artist once said that trifles make perfection, but 443
perfection is no trifle. This remark is as applicable to typing as it is 458
to art. You must constantly strive for excellence in order to become a 472
proficient typist. 476

| 1 | 2 | 3 | 4 | 5 | 6 | 7 | 8 | 9 | 10 | 11 | 12 | 13 | 14 | 15 |

Accuracy Study 11

Left Hand, First Finger

Goal: To enhance accuracy in typing by developing better control of the index finger of the left hand.

Features: These drills employ a systematic approach for mastering reaches involving the index finger. The words that have been selected not only contain a number of letters involving the forefinger but also reinforce specific, basic reaches on which many students make errors.

Line: 60 spaces

Directions: Type each line perfectly three times—not necessarily in succession, but in total. Begin a new line immediately when you make an error. Double-space between groups of three perfect lines. Begin each line slowly, and gradually increase your typing tempo.

Drill 1   R Stroke

rare rarefied rafts rascal rascally raze rasp raspberry rate
reach react reaction read reader rebate realize rebuke rebel
reciprocate reciprocity reflex reflexive regrets regrettable
resolute resolution respect retail retaliate restitute recur

Drill 2   F Stroke

fictitious fickle field figure figuration finances financial
frame frangible fray frazzle frank frankfurter freeze frozen
flux fly flurry fluffy foliage foil focal focalize foist fox
fed fender fencing festival fecund feed feeder fencer fervor

Drill 3   V Stroke

vellum vein venerable ventriloquist venture verb verbal very
vivid vivify vivisection vixen vizard vivacious vitiligo vat
visual visualize vision virulence virtue village villa vapid
valedictorian valiant valuate variate various variegated vex

Drill 4   T Stroke

tarp tarpaulin tar tarnish tape tapestry talk talking tactic
terminate terminal terrace terrestrial territory territorial
transaction transcend travel tranquil tranquility transcribe
transfer transferred traverse travesty tree treasurer treaty

During more than a quarter of a century, about ten thousand people 14
have learned the art of typewriting under my direct instruction. During 28
this period of time, there has not been one person who did not achieve this 43
facility, and this includes people from practically every background. 57

However, during my fifth year as an instructor, a young woman from 71
North Carolina entered our college. Her name was Ruth. She had been the 86
valedictorian of her high school class, and she also maintained an 99
excellent academic average at our school, except in the subject of 113
typewriting. It was my unfortunate duty to have to deny her a place on the 128
honor roll during her first year. She had the worst finger coordination 142
imaginable. It appeared that she could not get her fingers to cooperate 157
with her mind. Her self-respect was being slowly ground into oblivion. 172
Yet she was one of the hardest-working students we had. Despite all the 186
extraordinary efforts she put forth, it seemed that day by day she fell 201
further and further behind the class. 208

At the end of the school year, this overly anxious young woman asked 222
if she would ever learn to type well. For the first time in my life there 237
was an overwhelming impulse to tell someone that it was absolutely hopeless 252
and there was little chance that she would become a good typist. Her eyes, 268
large with apprehension, demanded the assurance that she could make it. 282
Although she would need a fighting spirit to conquer her obvious obstacles 297
and would have to exert extra effort, a special program was outlined for 312
her to follow during the summer. She was admonished to apply herself 326
completely to the job at hand, as this would enhance her chances of 339
success. 341

Not a defeatist by nature, Ruth practiced many hours each day during 355
the summer. No one knows how many hours, but it must have been a 368
tremendous number altogether. When Ruth returned to college in the autumn, 384
she not only had acquired excellent finger coordination but had developed a 399
considerable amount of speed and had achieved remarkable accuracy. At the 414
end of her second year, she received a gold medallion for being the 427
outstanding typist in the graduating class. 436

Here you have a story of a young woman who was at the bottom of her 450
class in typing the first year. However, she had an overwhelming desire to 465
be a good typist, and although she lacked the natural attributes, she 479
became the best in her class. So can you. 488

| 1 | 2 | 3 | 4 | 5 | 6 | 7 | 8 | 9 | 10 | 11 | 12 | 13 | 14 | 15 |

Accuracy Study 10

Shifting Drill

HANDS
STEADY

Goal: To improve accuracy in making capital letters.

Features: These drills contain a concentration of capital letters, which compel frequent shifting. Drills 3 and 4 are arranged so that the lines with the smallest number of capital letters are at the top of each drill, while those that contain the greatest number of capital letters are located at the bottom of each drill.

Line: 60 spaces

Drill Assignment: These assignments are for both Pretest/Posttest and Supplemental Diagnostic Tests. For Diagnostic Test 1, use Drill 1; for Diagnostic Test 2, use Drill 2; for Diagnostic Test 3, use Drill 3; for Diagnostic Test 4, use Drill 4; and for Diagnostic Test 5, use both Drill 3 and Drill 4. These directions apply only when you are doing corrective practice for the Diagnostic Tests as prescribed on Chart 3.

Directions: Type each line perfectly three times—not necessarily in succession, but in total. Begin a new line immediately when you make an error. Double-space between groups of three perfect lines. Begin typing each line slowly, and gradually increase your rate of speed. Type all four drills to correct faulty shifting. If your keyboard does not show the shift of the comma key as a comma and the shift of the period key as a period, do not depress shift when striking these keys in Drill 1, line 2.

Drill 1

```
aA ;: qQ pP sS lL wW oO dD kK eE iI fF jJ rR uU gG hH tT yY
aA ;: zZ /? sS lL xX .. dD kK cC ,, fF jJ vV mM gG hH bB nN
aA bB cC dD eE fF gG hH iI jJ kK lL mM nN oO pP qQ rR sS tT
uU vV wW xX yY zZ uU vV wW kK xX zZ mM aA nN bB mM cC oO gG
```

Drill 2 (Shift for each letter; do not use the shift lock.)

```
A : S L D K F J G H F J D K S L A : S L D K F J G H F J D K
S L A : S L D K F J G H F J D K S L A : S L D K F J G H F J
A : Q P A : Z ? S L W O S L X . D K E I D K C , F J R U F J
V M G H T Y G H B N F J R U F J V M D K E I D K C , S L W O
```

Drill 3

```
The Shifting For Capital Letters Is Very Tedious To Master.
Try To Spend Some Time Working On Your Major Problem Areas.
Typing Will Be Fun If You Go About It The Championship Way.
It Will Be A Great Skill If You Learn How To Shift Rapidly.
```

Drill 4

```
Much Skill Is Required To Learn How To Type Satisfactorily.
Mary Must Develop Perfect Timing In Order To Make Capitals.
It Is Not Easy Learning How To Type Rapidly And Accurately.
If You Want To Type Well, You Will Master This Phase Of It.
```

Words

A city is a study in contrasts. The rich, the poor, and the middle | 14
class dwell within its confines. Its varied architecture wears an air of | 29
perplexity as an ultramodern skyscraper rubs elbows with a Gothic | 42
cathedral, while across the street there is a parking lot with a wooden | 56
shed for the guard. And wide and splendid avenues cross undistinguished | 71
streets that dwindle off into back alleys. The city may seem cold and | 85
unfriendly, warm and enjoyable, an art center, a center of learning--it is | 100
all in the eye of the viewer. | 106

Actually it is all of these things and much more. A half hour's ride | 120
will transport one from the skyscrapers and crowds of the downtown area out | 135
to the farther reaches, where small houses and lawns and flower gardens are | 151
just as much a part of the metropolis as downtown is. Elsewhere, the city | 166
may have a shoreline, with beaches and fishing and all the amenities of a | 180
fine summer resort. One has only to choose. | 189

And always and everywhere there's the traffic. The first-time visitor | 204
gazes incredulously at the cars, the buses, and the trucks moving bumper to | 219
bumper through the city. Even the sophisticated city dweller perks an ear | 234
in the direction of a siren on a fire truck or ambulance pursuing its | 248
intrepid way through snarls of traffic. | 256

During the day, the city is the shopper's paradise, the worker's | 269
beehive, the banker's countinghouse. Twilight turns the sidewalks and | 283
streets into an elusive prairie stretching to the clifflike skyscrapers, | 298
and then the lights come on. Countless headlights and taillights in the | 313
roads shift and dart, the golden lights approaching, the red receding. | 327

Suddenly, the race is on. Like troops storming a beach, cavalcades of | 341
workers surge into the streets to get refuge in the subways, where, | 355
exhausted after a hard day's work, only the most agile find seats. The | 369
others stand, many trying hard to keep their balance by hanging on to the | 384
swaying straps overhead or on to metal handrails of a nearby seat. | 397

There seems to be little or no distinction as new vistas unfold. The | 412
night people swarm into the streets--pressing, pushing, and rushing to | 426
various places of entertainment. Once again there is the click of heels, | 441
the shuffling of feet, the glimmering of jewellike lights calling the | 455
passerby to places of entertainment. On the surface the city has become a | 470
fascinating world of glamour and luxury, but underneath, that view may be | 484
as unreal as a snow scene contained in a glass bubble. | 495

| 1 | 2 | 3 | 4 | 5 | 6 | 7 | 8 | 9 | 10 | 11 | 12 | 13 | 14 | 15

Drill 4　Right Hand

him dim pin kin no, to, do, so, pay say day may top mop pop
hymn pain lain rain main many body lady puny pony only baby
party hardy today sorry tardy dimly stick money honey carry
then them they pull hull dull maul doll hill bill will sill

Drill 5　Left Hand

act are bar bat sat ace was saw see sea tax few dew due far
here hear wear tear tact raze rear text bear bare faze fade
thing their there those where whose looks books beats beets
cares cease trace tract costs waste waxed seize right tight

Words

American Indians, of necessity, lived very systematic lives. The men   14
had certain functions and duties to perform just as the women had. The   29
fall and winter months were the busiest times of the year. During the   43
fall, the Indians gathered wild vegetables to be used during the cold   57
winter months, mended old clothes or made new clothing, and handcrafted   71
weapons for use in the winter hunting.   79

The Plains Indians depended chiefly on hunting for their food supply.   93
The regions teemed with wildlife--wild geese and ducks, prairie chickens,   108
turkeys, deer, and many other kinds of game. But by far the most important   123
game was buffalo. Each year the Indians killed thousands of buffaloes for   138
meat, clothing, bowstrings, harnesses, and tents. However, they killed   153
only what was needed. There was no indiscriminate slaughter.   165

Before starting on the winter hunt, the Indian chiefs and their braves   180
had to be in top physical condition. They needed tremendous stamina and   194
endurance to face the blizzards they were sure to encounter. With infinite   209
patience, these men, wearing snowshoes to aid their mobility, followed   224
footprints the animals made in the snow, until they overtook their prey.   238

Their picturesque homes, called tepees, were made of skins that were   252
placed on poles and had the appearance of giant inverted cones. The women   267
did most of the work in the camp. They prepared the meals, kept the tepee   282
clean, skinned and cleaned the animals that had been brought in by the   296
hunters, and made clothes from the tanned skins of the animals.   309

Summer was considered the best time of the year. It was a time of   323
festivities and celebrations. During this relaxed time, everyone forgot   337
the hardships and miseries faced during the previous winter.   350

This was the time when a brave entered into courtship. In some Indian   364
tribes, the courtship ritual was a fascinating experience for all involved.   379
At midnight, a brave courting a maiden would go to the tepee where she   394
lived with her parents. He would light a splinter of wood and hold it in   408
front of her face as he awakened her. If the girl did not find him a   422
pleasing suitor, she would ignore the flame and let it burn. This was her   437
way of rejecting his proposal. If she liked him, she would blow out the   452
flame, and he would ask her to become his wife. In an effort to gain the   467
acceptance of her parents, he would shower presents of blankets, ponies,   481
and other valuables upon them. Usually, the parents approved if their   496
daughter wished to marry the brave.   503

| 1 | 2 | 3 | 4 | 5 | 6 | 7 | 8 | 9 | 10 | 11 | 12 | 13 | 14 | 15 |

Accuracy Study 9

Spacing Drill

PALMS OF HANDS UP!

Goal: To improve accuracy in spacing between words and punctuation marks.

Features: These drills are composed of exercises in which it will be necessary to space after left- or right-hand strokes. Some of the drills require spacing after left-hand strokes, while others require spacing after right-hand strokes, and still other drills are a combination of the two. Each drill is labeled to facilitate identifying each type so that you can work on your particular spacing problem.

Line: 60 spaces

Drill Assignment: These assignments are for both Pretest/Posttest and Supplemental Diagnostic Tests. Determine whether you made more spacing errors after left- or right-hand strokes. Then do the appropriate drills. If most spacing errors were made after right-hand strokes, do Drill 1 and Drill 4. If too many spacing errors were made after left-hand strokes, do Drill 2 and Drill 5. If too many spacing errors were made after both left- and right-hand strokes, do Drill 3. *Always use your right thumb in spacing! Never use your left thumb.*

Directions: Type each line perfectly three times—not necessarily in succession, but in total. Begin a new line immediately when you make an error. Double-space between groups of three perfect lines.

Drill 1   Right Hand

```
; l k j h j k l ; l k j h j k l ; l k j h j k l ; l k j h j
p ; / o l . i k , u j m y h n u j m i k , o l . p ; / o l .
y h n u j m i k , o l . p ; / o l . i k , u j m y h n u j m
j u y h n m j u y h n m j u y h n m j u y h n m j u y h n m
```

Drill 2   Left Hand

```
a s d f g f d s a s d f g f d s a s d f g f d s a s d f g f
d s a s d f g f d s a s d f g f d s a s d f g f d s a s d f
q a z w s x e d c r f v t g b r f v e d c w s x q a z w s x
e d c r f v t g b r f v e d c w s x q a z w s x e d c r f v
```

Drill 3   Left and Right Hands

```
a b c d e f g h i j k l m n o p q r s t u v w x y z a b c d
e f g h i j k l m n o p q r s t u v w x y z a b c d e f g h
a ; q p s l w o d k e i f j r u g h t y f j r u d k e i s l
a ; z / s l x . d k c , f j v m g h b n f j v m d k c , s l
```

Words

A great deal has been written about champions in many fields, but 13
little has been written about champion typists. Since this book is about 28
championship typing techniques and methods, the characteristics found in 43
the rarest of all champions, the champion typists, will be considered. 57

It is an electrifying, motivating experience to watch a champion's 71
fingers flying over the keyboard at more than one hundred and sixty words a 86
minute without making a single error. There is nothing more dramatic to a 101
student than to observe a champion typist in action. 111

Champion typists are made; they are not born. However, there are some 126
indispensable qualities cultivated in a champion that distinguish that 140
individual from ordinary typists. There is a subtle combination of 154
ability, perception, perseverance, and dedication within the individual 168
that is augmented by the long, sometimes frustrating, and often tedious 182
hours, weeks, and even years of practice needed to reach the final goal. 197

The champion soon learns that technique is the major concern. What 211
may appear insignificant to an ordinary typist is of paramount importance 226
to a champion. The height of the chair or desk is a tremendous factor, 240
since one inch can make the difference of at least ten net words a minute. 255
A quick, firm striking of the keys is essential for speed. Fingers should 270
never linger on the keys, and fingers should be curved and hover close to 285
the keyboard. Incorrect stroking will result in errors and loss of speed. 300

So many different reaches are involved in typing that one must master 314
each one of them to avoid jerky motions or unnecessary pauses and to 328
develop smoothness and continuity in stroking. 337

Champions learned from conscientious practice. You, too, must utilize 352
your practice time to its best advantage if you wish to develop superior 366
typing skills. Striking the keys correctly is a technique which must be 381
developed before you can reach a high level of speed and accuracy. There 396
are several critical areas that you should emphasize: position of the 410
fingers, wrists, forearms, and elbows; touch; rhythm; and concentration. 425

Although you may spend your working day with fingers flying over a 438
keyboard, there are probably some mistakes you continue to make. These 453
problems must be attacked separately by analyzing each area and practicing 468
until the difficulty is eliminated. There is no substitute for proper 482
practice methods and techniques, so learn the championship way and start on 497
the road to high-speed typing. 503

| 1 | 2 | 3 | 4 | 5 | 6 | 7 | 8 | 9 | 10 | 11 | 12 | 13 | 14 | 15 |

Drill 22 V Stroke

vacate vacation vacuum vagabondage vagarious vagrant various
vagueness valve values valvular vampire vampirism vanquished
veal veer vegetable vegetate vehicles veiling velvety velvet
verse vest versus vertebra vertebras vertex vertexes vertigo

Drill 23 W Stroke

waste water waterer waterfall watt wave wax wavy waxy waiver
wear weak week wet wearily weapon weary weather weave weaver
wrangle wrap wrapped wrath wreak wrought wreathe wreck wrens
watch watchers watchful whack whacking whacky wrack wretched

Drill 24 X Stroke

xanthate xanthene xanthic xanthone xenias xerarch xylophones
xenophobe xenophobia xerography xylography xylem xylan axles
axe axes axile axiom axiomatic axis axle axenic axial auxins
auxiliary box boxes boxer boxy buxom exact exactly extremely

Drill 25 Y Stroke

yacht yachting yak yam yank yap yard yardage yawl yaws yield
yielding yip yipping yodel yodels yogurt yoke yokel yolk you
yore yonder your yourself young younger yoga youngster youth
yourselves youthful yowl yucca yule yurt yachts yipped yolks

Drill 26 Z Stroke

zabaglione zaffer zamia zanders zanily zaniness zany zagging
zeal zealot zealous zebra zebu zenith zenithal zeolite zooms
zephyr zero zeroes zest zesty zigs zigged zigging zigzagging
zigzag zigzagged zinc zincate zincite zinnia zinnias zoology

Section Five

Diagnostic Tests

Goal: To diagnose individual weaknesses in speed and/or accuracy.

Features: Each sentence emphasizes one particular type of problem area. The sentence number corresponds to the Accuracy Study or Speed Study number assigned for corrective practice. The Diagnostic Test number corresponds to the drill number within that Accuracy or Speed Study.

Line: 70 spaces

Word Wrap: OFF

Directions: Take a 1-minute timing on each of the ten specially constructed sentences. Key on a line-for-line basis. Begin each sentence on a new line. Key each sentence as many times as you can in 1 minute. Double-space between groups of sentences. Record results on Chart 3, following the directions on the chart.

Drill 16   P Stroke

physical physician physics physicist physiology physiography
pious piously pioneer pink pinnacle pip piping plunk plunger
polish police polo poll pole polemics public publicity puppy
pull pulmonary pulley pulpit pump pumpkin puny poliomyelitis

Drill 17   Q Stroke

quack quackery quad quadrangle quadrant quintet quinine quit
quaff quaffer quagmire quail quaint quake quale quick quaver
quality qualified qualification qualify qualitative quandary
quarrelsome query quarry quart quench quest quests questions

Drill 18   R Stroke

rabbi rabbit rabid rarity raccoon race racial racier rackets
racketeers radio radiator raffle raft rag ragged range razor
rebellion recap recast recede receded receipt receipts reply
revamp reveille reveal reverberate reverberant reverberation

Drill 19   S Stroke

seclude secret secretary seaweed sedge seesaw seize seizures
segregate sewage sextet sextuple sequence sequential squalid
staff stage stagger staples stapler starchy state statements
swag swagger swallow swampy swerve switch swell sweets swift

Drill 20   T Stroke

tatters tattered tattoos tattooer tawdry taverns taut taught
teach teachable technical technique technology teeter temper
trace tract trade traction tradition tragic tragedy transact
twist twister twitcher twinkle twirl twinge tweezer tweezers

Drill 21   U Stroke

ulcerous ulcerated ulterior ultimate ultimacy ultimatum unit
umbilicate umbilicus umbrage umbra umbrella umbrellas umpire
unconscious unconquerable unluckily unmanly unscrupulous use
upswing upstate uptake uranium upwards usable usage umpirage

Pretest/Posttest Diagnostic Test 1

ELBOWS AWAY FROM BODY

1 See if we can go and help them to do a fine job for the men and women.
2 Hostile conditions on the peninsula dissuaded them from the adventure.
3 Their neurotic visitor may bring down the six docks if he is not paid.
4 The pure vein of our silver was more than we had anticipated at first.
5 My annual bazaar grew swiftly and dazzled many overburdened lobbyists.
6 The bookkeeping committee from Tennessee embarrassed a football coach.
7 My nylon dress was the best garb she could wear to the bazaar at noon.
8 A quick movement of the bold enemy will jeopardize six good divisions.
9 I am to see if I am to do it now or if he is to do it at a later time.
10 It Is The Duty Of A King To Do Me A Turn If He Can And He Is To Do So.

| 1 | 2 | 3 | 4 | 5 | 6 | 7 | 8 | 9 | 10 | 11 | 12 | 13 | 14 |

Pretest/Posttest Diagnostic Test 2

1 This is a fine time to do some of the great things you may wish to do.
2 An improvement in clerical skills represents a helpful accomplishment.
3 Your ancient ivory emblem is an ornament to enrich and endow the city.
4 Whether they find more stores can make a big change in our selections.
5 A cold swan swiftly swam my brook and decided to dazzle its own flock.
6 An appellee cheerfully accommodated the aggressive coffee connoisseur.
7 The dazed bears raged in their cages as a lion slyly looked on nearby.
8 Extra work on psychology enabled five juniors to pass your major quiz.
9 It is the job of the aide to help me if he can and he is to do it now.
10 See If We Can Go With Them And Also Help To Do A Fine Job For The Men.

| 1 | 2 | 3 | 4 | 5 | 6 | 7 | 8 | 9 | 10 | 11 | 12 | 13 | 14 |

Pretest/Posttest Diagnostic Test 3

1 Now is the time for men and women to come to the aid of their country.
2 A sojourn on the highway provided us a pleasant respite from drudgery.
3 The authenticity of the proxy vote did torment the lame duck official.
4 Your piano will last as long as the quiet lady plays it in a fine way.
5 My umbrella survived a heartbreaking blizzard and innumerable hazards.
6 The committee from Mississippi suppressed a report from my bookkeeper.
7 Our well-fed polo pony only stared at a puny onion in his small stall.
8 The quiet preacher's texts just amazed forty very willing backsliders.
9 If it is up to me to do it, I am not for it at this or any other time.
10 Now And Then It Is True That We Can Do More Than We Thought If We Try.

| 1 | 2 | 3 | 4 | 5 | 6 | 7 | 8 | 9 | 10 | 11 | 12 | 13 | 14 |

MOVE FINGERS, NOT HANDS

Drill 10   J Stroke

jib jibe jiffy jig jigger jigsaw jitney jingle jink jive job
joist joke jokes joker journal jolly jolt josh jostle jovial
jugular juice juicer juicy jujitsu julep jumble jumpy jumper
junction juncture jungle junk jurisdiction juror justify joy

Drill 11   K Stroke

khaki khan kick kicker kid kidnap kidney kiss kowtow kernels
kill killer kiln kilocycle kilogram kilometer kimono killers
kind kindle kindly kindness kinescope kinetic kinetics knots
knead kneel knell knick knife knight know knowledge knuckles

Drill 12   L Stroke

liable liability liaison libel liberate limit liberation lie
load loaf loan lobby lobe lobster local locale location lock
loin loll lolly long look loop loom lower loon lowly loyalty
luminescent lump lunar lunatic lung lunge luster lurk lazily

Drill 13   M Stroke

maximum minimum milk mill militia militate military mind may
minnow minikin minimal minimize mink minister ministering my
mollify mollusk moment momentum monetize monk money monopoly
mummy mull mumps multiplicity mullion murmur murmurous money

Drill 14   N Stroke

numbs ninety nickel niece nibble nineteen nimble need needed
noise noisy nobility nocuous nomenclature nozzle nominations
nuance nuclear nucleus nudge null nullify numbers numerously
numinous nurture nuptial nursery nurse nylon night neighbors

Drill 15   O Stroke

oil oilily oiliness okra old oleomargarine olive olympic odd
oleographs olympiads ominously omelets ominous omnibus omega
omnificent omnipresent omnivorous once oneness onerous onion
opportunity oppose opposable opponent opposition opposite on

KEY WITH EASY RHYTHM.

Pretest/Posttest Diagnostic Test 4

1 Six men will come to the aid of the boys and girls of this fine store.
2 A naturalist was particularly concerned about substantial differences.
3 The proficiency of our neighbors did enchant and enrich their auditor.
4 I might take the option on the house if proper financing can be found.
5 The eccentric recluse decided to deduct innumerable gifts from my kin.
6 A buzzard effectively puzzled and dazzled the bobbing, hopping rabbit.
7 A puny puppy chased a fat, crazed cat in the grass area of the crater.
8 Zinnias, meekly vying for a bright effect, juxtaposed yellow jonquils.
9 See if it is to be done now or if we can do it all in the near future.
10 It Is I Who Will Have To Do Some Of The Things That I Will Not Do Now.

| 1 | 2 | 3 | 4 | 5 | 6 | 7 | 8 | 9 | 10 | 11 | 12 | 13 | 14 |

Pretest/Posttest Diagnostic Test 5

1 It is not what you do, but the way you do it that now counts the most.
2 Their combination of amusing anecdotes provided the proper atmosphere.
3 The dormant social problems did dismay our busy neighbor on the right.
4 There might be more jobs for everyone in the county if we plan for it.
5 Many hungry humans succeeded in surviving the unusually frigid autumn.
6 A pretty puppy appears to chase a raccoon into the hills successfully.
7 Your ill pupil fell into an oily pool as he dared to walk on its edge.
8 The quaint enzyme puzzled several exceptional judges before weakening.
9 A king is to do me a turn if he can as it is his sacred duty to do so.
10 It Is Up To You And Them To Find Out If Mary Is To Go To The Play Now.

| 1 | 2 | 3 | 4 | 5 | 6 | 7 | 8 | 9 | 10 | 11 | 12 | 13 | 14 |

Drill 4   D Stroke

dance dandruff danger dangle daze dazzled dazzling dare darn deacon debt dead deed deeded debacle debase debate debit dew decade decadent decedent decided deception decry desegregate drab draft drag dragging draw dragnet dragon dragoon drained

Drill 5   E Stroke

ebb ebony ebullience excelled excellent excellence eccentric ecclesiastic ecclesiastical echelon eczema ecdysis ecologist ego egocentric egoism equip equal equator equally equivalent evacuate evade evaporate evasive eve even event evolve extra

Drill 6   F Stroke

fable fabric facade face facet facetious fade fabulous fancy fear fearless feast feature federate felicity few fewer fend fracas fraction fragile fragmentary fragmentation fragrances fatal fatalistic fat fate fathom fateful fault fatuous favor

Drill 7   G Stroke

gab gabble gable gag gage gad gadfly gadget gaff gaffer gate gear geese geest great generic gelatinize gelatinous general gig giggle gigantic genius gift gilt ginger girl giraffe get graduate grain grand graze granite great greatest gregarious

Drill 8   H Stroke

hiatus hibernate high hill hilly him hilum hinder historical holiday holly holy home homely homonym homeroom homicide hop human humane humor humility humanity humanize humbug humdrum hydrants hybrid hydrogen hydrology hygiene hymn hypertension

Drill 9   I Stroke

iodic idiot iodine iodous ionic ionium ionize ionosphere ion imbricate imbroglio imitable imitate implication immediately indefatigability indefensibility individual input inimitable iniquity initiate initiation initiative injurious injustices

Supplemental Diagnostic Test 1

KEEP FEET FLAT ON THE FLOOR

1 It will be a good thing if you are able to keyboard this line quickly.
2 The sophisticated correspondent investigated many incompetent doctors.
3 The big man and rich girl did dispel the social rituals of their clan.
4 One thing that we can sing about now is how I can keystroke very well.
5 My jumpy friend grows more eccentric as he swiftly celebrates success.
6 Their tattooed football player accommodated his embarrassed roommates.
7 Our greatest cabbage exceeded minimum standards for edible vegetables.
8 You are very quickly whizzing through my text just by forced progress.
9 It is true that you can move your fingers fast when you wish to do so.
10 I Will Become Very Happy When You Can Stroke This Drill Fast And Well.

| 1 | 2 | 3 | 4 | 5 | 6 | 7 | 8 | 9 | 10 | 11 | 12 | 13 | 14 |

Supplemental Diagnostic Test 2

1 Now and then it is true that you can do well if you will do your best.
2 Our government ratified the restoration and refurbishment of the city.
3 Their ancient emblem dismays a tutor of airmen about its significance.
4 Our pet cats bit two boys and ran around the house very energetically.
5 A hazardous blizzard frequently injures many humans despite forecasts.
6 The careless innkeeper and successful beekeeper accommodated a friend.
7 My onion grew, in my opinion, only minimally in the desertlike cavern.
8 Six jumping zebras quickly hopped over nine of the fallen wildebeests.
9 It is up to you to strike as many keys as you can in order to do well.
10 Jan Must Practice This Drill With Great Care, And She Will Shift Well.

| 1 | 2 | 3 | 4 | 5 | 6 | 7 | 8 | 9 | 10 | 11 | 12 | 13 | 14 |

Supplemental Diagnostic Test 3

1 You must force yourself to key rapidly, as speed will not come to you.
2 Many managerial decisions require continual studies for effectiveness.
3 They may find the man and girl did do the ritual with flair and grace.
4 No one can imagine what the significance of these drills is right now.
5 Just decide to key these words slowly: minimum, frazzled, and browse.
6 The bookkeeping committees from Mississippi suppressed all statements.
7 My fat cat raced after my puny puppy and afterward deserted my garage.
8 A very few subjects were examined here and quickly recognized as poor.
9 I know you are happy to see so many small words that you can key well.
10 You Can Shift Very Fast In Keying This Drill If You Will Do Your Best.

| 1 | 2 | 3 | 4 | 5 | 6 | 7 | 8 | 9 | 10 | 11 | 12 | 13 | 14 |

Accuracy Study 8

Alphabetic Words

Goal: To enhance accuracy in typing by developing fluency in typing various letters of the alphabet.

Features: These drills employ a systematic approach for mastering a variety of strokes involving the entire alphabet and including the more difficult reaches on which most errors are made.

Line: 60 spaces

Drill Assignment: These assignments are for both Pretest/Posttest and Supplemental Diagnostic Tests. Determine which fingers were involved in making errors. Do drills for all fingers involved.

Directions: If you are typing corrective drills on one or several letters of the alphabet, type three perfect lines of each line—not necessarily in succession, but in total. Begin a new line immediately when you make an error. If you are to review the entire keyboard, type three perfect lines of the first two lines of each drill. If additional drills are necessary, type three perfect lines of the final two lines of each drill. Double-space between groups of three perfect lines.

Drill 1   A Stroke

abstracts abstractions abash abroad ability affects affected
are argue arguments agree agreement art arts artist artistry
avert averted avoidance avalanche avail availed availability
axone axiom axis axle axenic axial aqua aquarist aquiculture

Drill 2   B Stroke

batter battered badge badgered barren basin basket basketful
brown brought bring break breakfast brook brooks brand brain
be bees beat believe beware bewail between bewitch begin bet
basic basify base baseballs barrel barren bazooka barometers

Drill 3   C Stroke

cab cabaret cabbage cabin cabinet cable catch cactus captain
cease ceaseless cedar cede ceded ceil ceiling cell celebrate
crop crops crack cracker cradle craft crafty cram cramp cave
center central centric ceremony centipede certain cerebellum

Supplemental Diagnostic Test 4

KEEP EYES ON COPY

1 Keying a line with many small words will enable you to key with speed.
2 My meteorologist reported a substandard amount of precipitation today.
3 When the auditor did name the air corps for the problem, the maid hid.
4 Whether you play the piano or not, you must put out and walk the dogs.
5 The sweet fragrance of my azaleas dazzled the jumpy, greedy graduates.
6 The Tallahassee planning commission embarrassed the bookkeeping group.
7 My only nylon kimono was ragged and lumpy after washing in my hot tub.
8 Six quick brown foxes swiftly jumped over many hot, puny, lazy tigers.
9 You can key these small words at a fast pace if you wish to do so now.
10 Take Your Fingers Off The Home Row If You Have To Depress A Shift Key.

| 1 | 2 | 3 | 4 | 5 | 6 | 7 | 8 | 9 | 10 | 11 | 12 | 13 | 14 |

Supplemental Diagnostic Test 5

1 Speed will not come to you, so you must force yourself to key rapidly.
2 Many sociological implications required the ratification of the panel.
3 The pale prodigy from the land of the giant clams did fight for autos.
4 Your shop takes in more money in a month than most shops do in a year.
5 My jungle friend injured his brow swiftly swinging from a nearby tree.
6 A Tennessee buzzard attacked a hopping, bobbing rabbit for its dinner.
7 A dazed, battered crab crawled eastward and westward up the only hill.
8 My jazz expert quickly jumped very willingly from the bandstand today.
9 It will be to your benefit if you can key small words at a good speed.
10 One Of The Most Difficult Skills Is To Be Able To Shift Very Fluently.

| 1 | 2 | 3 | 4 | 5 | 6 | 7 | 8 | 9 | 10 | 11 | 12 | 13 | 14 |

Drill 4   M, N, O, and P

minimum milk milium mink minikin monopoly mummy mull milium
nip nylon noon nook null nun nylon ninny null no nylon nook
oil oilily onion only opinion oil oilily onion only opinion
pin pip plunk polo polio pulp pull pumpkin puppy pony pulpy

Drill 5   R, S, T, and V

raze raft ragged rare rate react recede rebate reverberates
saw savage saber seaweed stab scarf seesaw starve segregate
tattered tax tract teeter terse trace tweezer tweezers text
vacate vat veer vegetate vested verse vertebra vex vertexes

Drill 6   W, X, Y, and Z

wade wader wafer waft wafter wag ward war ware was wear wet
weave web weft west wrest wart wasted waterers watered wave
union you extra extracted sextet union you extra exaggerate
zebra zest zed zagged zebra zest zag zagged zebra zag zebra

Section Six

Skill-Development Paragraphs

Goal: To develop speed and accuracy in typing ordinary paragraphs for a period of 1 minute.

Features: These paragraphs contain a large number of common words, with a balanced concentration of various stroke combinations. Each succeeding paragraph is increased in length by 5 words, thereby requiring greater speed with perfect accuracy.

Line: 75 spaces

Word Wrap: ON

Directions: Type each paragraph within 1 minute without making a single error, beginning with the 20-word paragraph and progressing as far as you can.

Accuracy Study 7

One-Hand Words

Goal: To increase accuracy in typing one-hand words.

Features: These drills are composed of one-hand words so that fluency can be developed in typing them. One-hand words are very difficult to type and are typed at a slower rate of speed than most other words. These drills are arranged alphabetically to facilitate locating particular letter combinations for corrective drilling.

Line: 60 spaces

Drill Assignment: These assignments are for both Pretest/Posttest and Supplemental Diagnostic Tests. For Diagnostic Test 1, use Drill 1; for Diagnostic Test 2, use Drill 2; for Diagnostic Test 3, use Drill 3; for Diagnostic Test 4, use Drill 4; and for Diagnostic Test 5, use both Drill 5 and Drill 6. These directions apply only when you are doing corrective practice for the Diagnostic Tests as prescribed on Chart 3.

Directions: Type each line perfectly three times—not necessarily in succession, but in total. Begin a new line immediately when you make an error. Double-space between groups of three perfect lines. Type all six drills if you have problems typing one-hand words. Otherwise, if you can identify a particular type of one-hand word that gives you difficulty, concentrate on that particular corrective drill. For example, if one-hand words on the right side of the keyboard cause you a great deal of difficulty, practice only those words in which the letters are located on the right side of the keyboard.

Drill 1   A, B, C, and D

abate abstracter affected acts are agree aware axe avert as

battered badgered bar base bees beware better beg bear best

cabaret cabbage cage cad cease cedar crab craft cast caters

dab dad daze dare debt deeded debase decade drab draw dress

Drill 2   E, F, G, and H

eager ease east ebb edge eggs ersatz ewe eve evade exceeded

facade fade far fear federate fewer fever fat fracas feeder

gadget gaffer gage gate gas gaze gear geese geezer greatest

hill hilly him hilum hip hippy hokum holly holy hilly hippy

Drill 3   I, J, K, and L

ill ilium ilk imply ink ionium ion inky ill ink imply ilium

jink jolly jump junk jumpy junky join joy junky jolly jumpy

kill kiln kimono kin kink kip kill kiln kimono kin kink kip

lily limp loin loll lolly look loop loom loon lull lip look

20 Words

Knowing what to type as well as how to type will make it possible for you to become a very good typist.

25 Words

If you are energetic and if you will follow instructions, you will enjoy typing. You will also acquire a very important skill.

30 Words

Typing can be fun. All you have to do is concentrate on developing championship typing techniques, and if you succeed, you will really love to type.

35 Words

Now you have learned the location of the keys on the keyboard. Your future progress will depend upon your practicing the right drills in the right way. Key as you have been told.

40 Words

Students who put forth their best effort in learning to type find that they do much better than other students. Therefore, give typing the very best you have, and the very best will come back to you.

Accuracy Study 6

Double-Letter Words

Goal: To enhance accuracy in typing double-letter words.

Features: These drills contain many words possessing double letters. Double-letter strokes are among the slowest strokes in typing. The drills are arranged in alphabetic sequence.

Line: 61 spaces

Drill Assignment: These assignments are for both Pretest/Posttest and Supplemental Diagnostic Tests. For Diagnostic Test 1, use Drill 1; for Diagnostic Test 2, use Drill 2; for Diagnostic Test 3, use Drill 3; for Diagnostic Test 4, use Drill 4; and for Diagnostic Test 5, use both Drill 1 and Drill 4.

Directions: Type each line perfectly three times—not necessarily in succession, but in total. Begin a new line immediately when you make an error. Double-space between groups of three perfect lines. Type all four drills if you have problems making double-letter strokes.

Drill 1   A, B, C, and D
```
aardvark aardwolf Aaron Aaronic bazaar aardvark Aaron bazaars
bubble ebb rabbit bobbing robber hobby gobble bobbing bubbles
succeed occasion account accompany accrue occurs successfully
add middle forbidden adduce fiddler addition adding forbidden
```

Drill 2   E, F, G, and L
```
feel heel steel bleed engineer three sweet breeze beef degree
effect coffee differ difficult off affluent efforts officials
bragging dagger luggage baggage suggest struggling braggingly
dollar ball all bull rally allege parallel hall all fill well
```

Drill 3   M, N, O, and P
```
recommend summary communicate comment programmers commitments
planner running winning skinny dinner planned connect sinners
too boom book coordinate broom cool brook zoom look root boot
appear supply opportunity wrapped suppress appraise appraised
```

Drill 4   R, S, T, and Z
```
horror embarrassment worry error corruption current embarrass
class pressure assume assail grass assassination essence pass
pretty attention ghetto attrition attack attract utter better
jazz buzzard puzzles dazzle embezzlement blizzards embezzling
```

45 Words

No matter what your goal in typing is, there is one fact you must realize: a keyboard will reflect only the energy and desire that you put into it. If you will not do anything, the keyboard will do the same, so do your best.

50 Words

To type accurately, you must develop the habit of analyzing each error, recording each on your error-analysis chart, and exercising care not to make that error again. If you will follow the corrective measures outlined, you will type more accurately.

55 Words

One of the important questions you have to answer right now is whether you will expend the energy it takes to master typing. You are following the trail of champions, and you will save yourself a great deal of frustration by conscientiously doing what you are instructed.

60 Words

One of the proudest moments in my life was the first time I was able to type sixty words in a minute without making any errors. You are at the brink of discovering this marvelous feeling. In order to accomplish this feat, you must type at the rate of five strokes a second without making any errors.

65 Words

It is a fascinating thing to observe one who is able to type fast and accurately. It means that this individual has spent time mastering the right way to do all of the operations in typing and has also followed a carefully designed skill-development program to develop superior typing skills. That is what you are doing now.

Drill 10   J Finger

umbel umbilicate umbilicus umbrage umbrageous umbrella umbra
immunologist immune tumultuously inhumanity autumnal jumpers
unabated unabridged unaccustomed unavailable uncouth uncruel
unhurried unused unusually unutterable unyielding unnumbered

Drill 11   K Finger

kibitz kibitzer kick kickers kidnap kidnapper kidney killers
killer kilogram kingdom kilt kimono kind kindle kindred king
kitchen kite kitty kitchenette kinescope kinematics kilogram
kindergarten kin kindred kill kinetic kiss kidskin kingcraft

Drill 12   L Finger

load loaf loan lobby lobsters lockers locomotive logarithmic
logic logistic lonesome long longevity longitude loopy lowly
color follow hollow folders oleander soliloquy oleomargarine
hold fold told cold sold bold gold old stole whole hole mole

70 Words

You cannot become proficient in typing unless you have a positive attitude. Therefore, each time you sit at your keyboard you should believe that you are going to do some wonderful typing today. If you really believe in yourself, you will find that you will type rapidly and accurately, so have confidence in yourself and you will progress steadily.

75 Words

KEY LETTER FOR LETTER

You must maintain a steady tempo in typing in order to type fast. I have seen many people type rapidly in spurts only to lose the speed advantage made in the spurt by a long pause--during which the typist endeavors to line the fingers in position to type the next word. A pause robs you of speed, so do not pause. You must keep your fingers close to the keys to increase speed.

80 Words

Success in typewriting is usually the result of doing the right thing, in the right way, with zest and regularity. This is why it is vitally important that you type a certain way. The importance of good typing habits cannot be overemphasized. Each drill in this book has been carefully and scientifically planned to provide you with a systematic development of typing skills to guarantee success.

85 Words

Each time you are able to type one of these paragraphs, which are getting longer and more difficult to type, without making an error, you have climbed another rung up the ladder of success. I am certain that you are very proud of what you have been able to accomplish and are now looking forward to typing this paragraph perfectly, then the next, and the next, until you are able to type the one-hundred-word paragraph.

Drill 4   F Finger

```
friend from frame fruit fragrance fragment fragile fractures
craft raft draft swift lift rift drift left soft shaft often
break brake braggart braggadocio bravo bramble brass brought
bring brannigan brave brawl bread breach breast broil bruise
```

Drill 5   F Finger

```
grab grabble grace gracious gradate graduate graft graduates
ground great gray gruesome greed gregarious grievance gritty
grip grippe grist grizzle groom grocery growling grain gross
groove ground growth growling grove grotesque grotto grudges
```

Drill 6   J Finger

```
jump jumpy just justly jumble jumper junction juncture junky
jungle junior junk juniper junket junta junto jurat justices
injure injury injurious injuriousness injunction injudicious
injustice inject injector injectable injudiciousness injects
```

Drill 7   J Finger

```
hub huddle hues hued huff huffy hug huckster huge humorously
human humanism humanity humanize humble humid humor humorous
hyaline hyalite hybrid hydrant hydraulic hydrogen hydroplane
hypnotic hymn hymnal hypnosis hypnotism hyphen hypercritical
```

Drill 8   J Finger

```
much mucilage muciferous muck mucus mud muddy muffler muffin
tumble jumble mumble stumble rumble fumble humble jumble rum
myoglobin myrrh myself mystery mystic mystify mythologically
myopia mycology myasthenia musty musket music mustard museum
```

Drill 9   J Finger

```
numeration nuncupative nuptial numerology numerous numerator
nuance nub nuclear nucleus nudge nullify nuisance number nut
nylons any many anyway anytime anything synonymous gymnasium
nun numb nuncle numerical numismatic numismatically nummular
```

90 Words

CONCENTRATE!

I have taught many students to type ninety or more words a minute without making a single error. Of course, it does require a great deal of discipline--both mental and physical. It is important that you have the capacity for hard work because it will take a great deal of determination on your part to continue to progress from paragraph to paragraph. It will probably be necessary for you to consult with your teacher regularly for typing tips.

95 Words

There is a definite correlation between what you are able to type speedwise on these one-minute paragraphs and your net speed on a five-minute timed writing. You will see that as you improve your speed on these one-minute paragraphs, so will your speed increase on the five-minute timed writings. Therefore, by developing your speed on these paragraphs, you will simultaneously and rapidly improve your productivity on longer timed writings. Practice these drills every day.

100 Words

One of the finest feelings you will ever experience will be the first time you are able to type one hundred words a minute perfectly. I wish I could find adequate words to express the exhilaration you will feel once you are able to type this paragraph in a minute without an error. I know that the first time I typed perfectly at that rate was one of the happiest days of my life. You are close to experiencing this wonderful sensation, and if you are successful, you will be considered an expert typist.

Accuracy Study 5

Vertical-Stroke Words

KEY WITH EASY RHYTHM

Goal: To increase accuracy in typing vertical-stroke words.

Features: These drills contain a concentration of vertical-stroke words. A vertical stroke is made when one finger has to strike two or more consecutive keys on different rows of the keyboard. Example: *raze,* in which the letters *az* are struck by the A finger consecutively. Vertical strokes are among the slowest in typing, and a great deal of practice is required to develop fluency in typing them. These drills are arranged so that the first drill concentrates on vertical strokes beginning with the A finger and progresses from left to right to the L finger.

Line: 60 spaces

Drill Assignment: These assignments are for both Pretest/Posttest and Supplemental Diagnostic Tests. Determine which fingers were involved in making errors. Do drills for all fingers involved.

Directions: Type each line perfectly three times—not necessarily in succession, but in total. Begin a new line immediately when you make an error. Double-space between groups of three perfect lines.

Drill 1   A Finger

```
aquacade aqualungs aquamarines aquaplanes aquarelle aquatint
azaleas azide azimuths azine azo azoic azonal azoth azoturia
jazz dazzle hazard haze razor bazaar jazz dazzle raze razors
buzzard hazard lizard blizzard pizza bazaar buzzard blizzard
```

Drill 2   S Finger

```
swat swear sweet sword sweep swell swift sway swap swanskins
swamp sweat swallow swindle swing swollen swizzle swim swing
blows flows lows laws blows saws views flaws paws news brews
flows frowns slows sews sows grows brows bows tows cows rows
```

Drill 3   D Finger

```
ceded cedar cecum ceiling celebrate celebrity celery censure
deeded decedent deceased deceit decelerate deceive deception
eccentric ecclesiastic ecology eclipses economy ecstasy echo
educate education educe editor editorial edition edify edict
```

**KEEP EYES
ON COPY**

You have now reached the point in your typing development where you are considered a typing expert. It will become increasingly difficult for you to type each of the succeeding paragraphs, as each is longer than the preceding one, and it will be much more difficult to type. In order to progress, you must decide to work more diligently than you ever did before in order to continue your upward climb in typing proficiency. You will find that what is true in the field of typing is also true in other fields of endeavor.

110 Words

As you press onward for higher speeds, you will find that more and more errors will occur initially. This is due to several reasons. First, you have more words on which you can make errors. Secondly, your fingers have to move at an incredible rate of speed. Also, you are beginning to become more tense because you have to type so many words without making an error. However, if you do not become discouraged and practice these paragraphs diligently, you will notice that your accuracy will improve daily and soon all of your errors will be gone.

115 Words

At this point you should be able to type straight copy at the rate of ninety net words a minute on five-minute writings. You should now have excellent finger control and be a very productive typist. Of equal importance, however, is your ability to get along well with others. After all, you must work with others, and in order to achieve success in life, you must be able to work harmoniously with others. To achieve success is why you have worked so diligently on your typing, and you must work just as diligently on developing your personal relations with others.

Accuracy Study 4

Compound- and Multiple-Stroke Words

ARMS AND WRISTS STEADY

Goal: To increase accuracy in typing compound- and multiple-stroke words.

Features: These drills are composed of compound- and multiple-stroke words. A compound stroke is one in which two or more consecutive strokes are made by two or more different fingers of the same hand; for example: *point,* in which the letters *poin* are struck by the fingers of the right hand consecutively. A multiple stroke takes place when two compound strokes involving both hands occur in one word. Example: *most,* which involves two fingers of the right hand, followed by two fingers of the left hand.

Line: 60 spaces

Drill Assignment: These assignments are for both Pretest/Posttest and Supplemental Diagnostic Tests. For Diagnostic Test 1, use Drill 1; for Diagnostic Test 2, use Drill 2; for Diagnostic Test 3, use Drill 3; for Diagnostic Test 4, use Drill 4; and for Diagnostic Test 5, use both Drill 1 and Drill 4.

Directions: Type each line perfectly three times—not necessarily in succession, but in total. Begin a new line immediately when you make an error. Double-space between groups of three perfect lines.

Drill 1

```
lag hag nag toy coy had ban dam ram now out won win tin bin
dim pit hid has hat hot not let new who two boy hit his mat
nip sin lie tap our can pot put pat say ran van day fan tan
her way new few hat hot ton one tip top pet cap pit set ran
```

Drill 2

```
lies time sail fail wail rail fine cost find bout rout talk
walk what main mean cure pure view pose fair fine find file
vein rein rain sure shop ship take more live this stop mire
most jobs mast past last luck pick post cast mast lost rose
```

Drill 3

```
knack poise ration endure daily option quite quiet might be
begin piano person there where whether ignore ignite tempts
paint power lower flower tower personality personal persons
that more thing weevils wings confrontation singing ringing
```

Drill 4

```
serious combination fundamental institutions advantage were
information pursuits perhaps inspiration financial pictures
influence imagination available achievement everything that
let general vindication around someone conscious stupendous
```

You have spent a considerable amount of time and put forth a tremendous effort to reach this level of typing proficiency. I know you are exceedingly proud of your accomplishments, as only a few typists are able to type straight copy at this rate of speed without making an error. I am also proud of you because I know you have paid your dues. It has taken an extraordinary amount of personal dedication and discipline to reach this level of excellence. What you have learned in typing can be applied in all of your endeavors and will produce very gratifying results. It has worked for me.

125 Words

I know you are wondering if it is possible for you to make your fingers go fast and accurately enough so you can complete this paragraph in a minute. You know how difficult it has been for you to complete the preceding paragraph. It will be much more difficult to type this one satisfactorily. Therefore, make up your mind that you will have to expend a great deal of energy and that it will require a great deal of determination in order to succeed. You must also be able to relax completely so you will not become too tense. Tenseness is your greatest enemy when speed-typing. Therefore, think positive and relax.

130 Words

You have reached the last paragraph in these progressive speed drills. You have now reached the championship class among typists and have acquired the digital dexterity that only a few typists have mastered. It will tax all of your energy, determination, tenacity, and positive thinking in order to type this paragraph in a minute without an error. If you are successful, you will have a most satisfying experience, because you will realize that you have joined a select group of typists, those who can type very rapidly and accurately. You are on your way to a level of typing proficiency that will amaze and please others as well as yourself.

Drill 4

span make dory paid worn torn mend half prod dock ogle pend
mend lend envy odor maid paid laid pair lair hair chap burn
turn curl fury firm lake bush lays idle rosy dish isle risk
halt iris wish fish male form goal dual gory dial hale also

Drill 5

profit icicle sleigh emblem sicken quench lament clench she
shame quake shake flair tight fight sight tithe eight widow
bigot blend usual digit audit spend amend fiend penal slept
amble bugle endow whale focus title shale cycle chair autos

Section Seven

Accuracy Studies

Goal: To provide practice on drills specially constructed to promote accuracy.

Features: These accuracy studies are constructed to emphasize particular stroke combinations.

1. Simple-Vocabulary Words
2. High-Stroke-Intensity Words
3. Alternate-Hand Words
4. Compound- and Multiple-Stroke Words
5. Vertical-Stroke Words
6. Double-Letter Words
7. One-Hand Words
8. Alphabetic Words
9. Spacing Drill
10. Shifting Drill
11. Left Hand, First Finger
12. Right Hand, First Finger
13. Left Hand, Second Finger
14. Right Hand, Second Finger
15. Left Hand, Third Finger
16. Right Hand, Third Finger
17. Left Hand, Fourth Finger
18. Right Hand, Fourth Finger
19. Left-Hand Words
20. Right-Hand Words
21. Punctuation
22. Concentration Drills—Similar Words
23. Concentration Drills—Long Words
24. Concentration Drills—Unusual Words
25. Intensive Concentration Drills—Paragraphs
26. Concentration Drills—Split Doublets
27. Intensive Concentration Drills—Reverse Typing

Line: Varies

Word Wrap: OFF

Directions: Follow the directions for each study.

Accuracy Study 3

Alternate-Hand Words

Goal: To increase accuracy in typing alternate-hand words.

Features: These drills are composed of alternate-hand words.

Line: 60 spaces

Drill Assignment: These assignments are for both Pretest/Posttest and Supplemental Diagnostic Tests. For Diagnostic Test 1, use Drill 1; for Diagnostic Test 2, use Drill 2; for Diagnostic Test 3, use Drill 3; for Diagnostic Test 4, use Drill 4; and for Diagnostic Test 5, use Drill 5.

Directions: Type each line perfectly three times—not necessarily in succession, but in total. Begin a new line immediately when you make an error. Double-space between groups of three perfect lines.

Drill 1

```
it rod when with right angle social ancient antique quantity
is the city them sight fight vivify emblems dormant fiendish
of aid than then chaps chant dismal visitor auditor sorority
to and when turn bogus blame mantle proviso visible neighbor
```

Drill 2

```
do got girl duty giant handy island prodigy problem ornament
so row wish hand flame right shanty audible enchant clemency
if man roam clan civic forms panels suspend element toxicity
an roe hang dirk their gowns formal rituals augment mementos
```

Drill 3

```
am men they rich girls corps ritual figment torment neurotic
by may pale both vigor clams burial socials emblems rigidity
us for busy down ivory tutor disown dispels formals problems
he did name lane world usual airmen disowns rituals provisos
```

Accuracy Study 1

Simple-Vocabulary Words

**CENTER BODY
TO KEYBOARD**

Goal: To increase accuracy in typing short words.

Features: These drills contain a concentration of short words.

Line: 60 spaces

Drill Assignment: The assignments are for both Pretest/Posttest and Supplemental Diagnostic Tests. For Diagnostic Test 1, use Drill 1; for Diagnostic Test 2, use Drill 2; for Diagnostic Test 3, use Drill 3; for Diagnostic Test 4, use Drill 4; and for Diagnostic Test 5, use both Drills 1 and 5.

Directions: Type each line perfectly three times—not necessarily in succession, but in total. If you make an error in typing a line, begin a new line immediately. After you have typed the first line perfectly three times, double-space and begin the second line. Double-space between groups of three perfect lines. Begin typing slowly and increase your speed gradually.

Drill 1

```
in to of is to go do on it at so an if he we us as up or be
and men the six aid boy our you out pit now see not but way
can run dog get fox day too two may man one for aid due top
are her she him two put hot big for our ten dad ran won how
```

Drill 2

```
one but yet try who all put sit set own pay out lay say day
more moor will well wail vote vast vest best boat this that
then than them they work come came year hear here boys girl
toys file tile dial pile mile rile sail sale some dome zone
```

Drill 3

```
lone loan time fine find mine mind pine wind wine nine bind
must dust just guts gust rust type fast last cast mast past
make take lake bake rake wake cake sake like bike kite mike
dike pike what when whom call coil hall hail hale here hear
```

Drill 5

```
cohesiveness interpreting partisanship insensitivity nostalgically
superstition veterinarian disastrously nutritionists healthfulness
recognizance incapacitate continuances revolutionary instinctively
evangelizing effervescent metaphysical intravenously meteorologist
```

Drill 6

```
rhapsodizing machinations discomfiture hallucination indefatigable
condominiums persuasively successfully possibilities disseminating
postponement extravaganza interminable preoccupation improprieties
ecstatically monopolistic inflationary automatically vilifications
```

Drill 7

```
restaurateur misdemeanors masquerading confrontation intransigence
exorbitantly enshrinement preposterous intentionally unprecedented
entrepreneur embezzlement precariously realistically admissibility
gratuitously abstruseness transcendent manipulations gubernatorial
```

Drill 8

```
usuriousness codification abbreviation interceptions diametrically
legitimizing mobilization recalcitrant irresponsible fictionalized
complexities deficiencies unquenchable deductibility electrocution
excoriations unregenerate inconsolable immunologists unflinchingly
```

Drill 9

```
fulminations loquaciously lexicography parenthetical biorhythmical
excruciating insinuations melodramatic fundamentally protectionism
lasciviously presumptuous editorialize choreographer topographical
sporadically symbolically jeopardizing precipitously spontaneously
```

Drill 10

```
teleprinters sociological budgeteering colonizations anachronistic
visibilities accumulating implications consciousness embarrassment
irreversible enthusiastic ratification bureaucracies collaborative
superstellar abstractions characterize preponderance tantalizingly
```

Drill 4

city near past does fast slow with best true very want work
give have seek fact like folk help jobs much lack fail task
hard each must went need help down whom fine what paid face
lift many wish will days turn mind once with rate feel find

Drill 5

most mast mere deer dear tear hare hard hair well sell fell
feel kill hill till fill peel pare pear pull pool poll than
away your year many good wood hood food mood mode node noll
turn down ship west east rain feet walk soul sole keys sold

Accuracy Study 2

High-Stroke-Intensity Words

Goal: To increase accuracy in typing long words.

Features: These drills contain a concentration of long words.

Line: 70 spaces

Drill Assignment: These assignments are for both Pretest/Posttest and Supplemental Diagnostic Tests. For Diagnostic Test 1, use Drill 1 and Drill 6; for Diagnostic Test 2, use Drill 2 and Drill 7; for Diagnostic Test 3, use Drill 3 and Drill 8; for Diagnostic Test 4, use Drill 4 and Drill 9; and for Diagnostic Test 5, use Drill 5 and Drill 10.

Directions: Type each line perfectly three times—not necessarily in succession, but in total. Begin a new line immediately when you make an error. Double-space between groups of three perfect lines. Begin typing each line slowly, and gradually increase your typing rate as you get familiar with the line of writing.

Drill 1

```
calisthenics disconcerted questionable introspection surreptitious
subordinates compromising precipitated systematizing idiosyncratic
contaminated journalistic inconsistent complementing psychodynamic
hyperkinetic degenerative partitioning transgression therapeutical
```

Drill 2

```
ecumenically undercurrent disruptively retrospective psychotherapy
undercurrent distractions expeditional abnormalities squeamishness
totalitarian professional underdevelop precipitation proselytizing
uproariously pediatrician perseverance recrimination catalytically
```

Drill 3

```
eccentricity incarcerated abridgements methodologies paradoxically
convergences malnutrition arithmetical psychological schizophrenic
antithetical unauthorized tractability opportunistic interspersing
predilection unassailable decisiveness compassionate expeditionary
```

Drill 4

```
disseminated increasingly elucidations flexibilities acrimoniously
universality disconnected dictatorship authorization jurisdictions
encyclopedia unofficially optimistical sophisticated certification
peripherally explications artificially investigative resuscitation
```